THE GRAND BAZAAR
KAPALI ÇARŞI

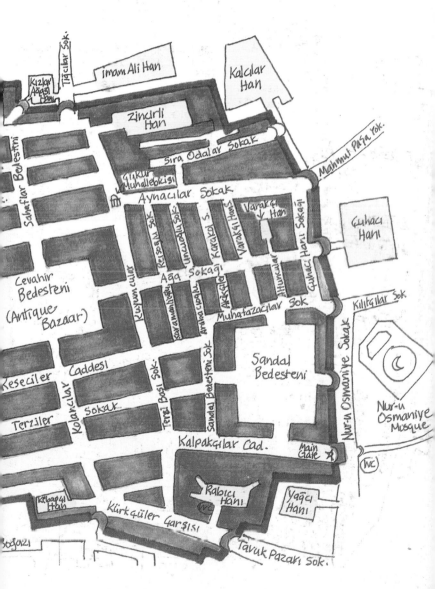

Tüccılar Sok.

İmam Ali Han

Kalcılar Han

Kızlar Ağası Han

Zincirli Han

Sıra Odalar Sokak

Mahmut Paşa Yok.

Sahaflar Bedesteni

Çukur Muhallebicisi

Aynacılar Sokak

Varakçı Han

Çuhacı Hanı

Reisoğlu Sok.

Umculoğlu Sok.

Karakol S.

Varakçı Hanı S.

Çuhacı Hanı Sokağı

Kılıtçılar Sok

Cevahir Bedesteni

(Antique Bazaar)

Kuyumcular

Ağa Sokağı

Sayamanhalığ

Akkoçeler

Arabacı Sok

Muhafazacılar Sok

Kilitçiler Sok

Nur-u Osmaniye Sokak

Kesecilar Caddesi

Kolancılar Sokak

Terzi Başı Sok.

Sandal Bedesteni Sok.

Sandal Bedesteni

Nur-u Osmaniye Mosque

Terziler

Kalpakçılar Cad.

Main Gate

wc

Kebapçı Han

Rabıcı Hanı

Yağcı Hanı

wc

Kürkçüler Çarşısı

Boğazı

Tavuk Pazarı Sok.

Istanbul's Bazaar Quarter:
BACKSTREET WALKING TOURS

Ann Marie Mershon and
Edda Renker Weissenbacher
Photographs: Ann Marie Mershon

Istanbul's Bazaar Quarter:
BACKSTREET WALKING TOURS

Ann Marie Mershon and
Edda Renker Weissenbacher
Photographs: Ann Marie Mershon

Library of Congress Cataloging-in-Publication Data

Mershon, Ann Marie
   Istanbul's bazaar quarter: backstreet walking tours / Ann Marie Mershon,
Edda Renker Weissenbacher
Istanbul: Çitlembik Publications, 2009.
182 p.: photo., map.; 12.5x21.5 cm
ISBN: 978-9944-424-59-2

1. Istanbul (Turkey)–Description and travel.
2. Istanbul (Turkey)–Antiquities
3. Bazaars (Markets)–Turkey–Istanbul.
I.Title. 2.Weissenbacher, Edda Renker

LC: DR726
DC: 949.618

Photographs: Ann Marie Mershon, Murat Oğurlu
Page Layout: Çiğdem Dilbaz

Printed and Binding:
Mart Matbaacılık Sanatları
Mart Plaza, Merkez Mah. Ceylan Sok.
No: 24 Nurtepe, İstanbul
Tel: +90 212 321 23 00

In Turkey:
Çitlembik Publications
Şehbender Sokak 18/4
Asmalımescit-Tünel
34430 Istanbul TURKEY
www.citlembik.com.tr
kitap@citlembik.com.tr

In the USA:
Nettleberry, LLC.
44030 123rd St.
Eden, South Dakota 57232
www.nettleberry.com

Contents

Acknowledgments

I thank Tania Chandler and Jamilah Lajam, who introduced me to Edda, I thank Edda and the friends who encouraged her, and I thank Nancy Özturk at Çitlembik for having faith in our collective dream.

And, of course, I thank Istanbul for its charm, its culture, and its rich history.

Ann Marie Mershon

And I, Edda, would like to thank our talented and cheerful Ann Marie from the bottom of my heart for motivating me to share in the making of this book. It has been a great pleasure working with her.

Edda Renker Weissenbacher

Ann Marie Mershon Discovers Edda's Istanbul

Ann Marie didn't discover Istanbul until her mid-50's, when she took a teaching position at the Koç High School. Those two years launched her into a love affair with Istanbul, with its unique history and fascinating culture.

As a lifetime resident of Minnesota, her passion for outdoor adventure had been the focus of her writing. She published magazine articles and newspaper columns about health, fitness, travel, and a myriad of outdoor activities. In 2004 she published a children's historical novel, *Britta's Journey, An Emigration Saga*.

Ann Marie has two grown sons who live in Florida, but she chooses to stay in her northwoods home near the Canadian border where Lake

Superior and the Boundary Waters Canoe area have been her play-ground. As she often tells curious Turks, "Grand Marais is the Antalya of Minnesota." Its awe-inspiring natural beauty is certainly picturesque, but it lacks the captivating history of Istanbul.

As an English teacher, Ann Marie traveled extensively overseas with student groups, although a brief stop at Ephesus on a Greek Island tour was all she'd seen of Turkey before she accepted the teaching position at Koç.

Launching herself whole-heartedly into the experience of teaching English to Turkish students, Ann Marie also devoted every free weekend to exploring her new home. She quickly developed a love for Istanbul's ferryboats as she wandered Kadıköy, Taksim, Sultanahmet, and Eyüp. She snapped countless photos and included them with lengthy e-mails (later blogs) about her experiences in and around Turkey. One of Ann Marie's most treasured finds was Edda Renker Weissenbacher, who guided friends through the back streets of Istanbul, entertaining them with tales of the city's history. Ann Marie introduced her own friends to Edda. Enlightened and enthused by their shared enthusiasm, Ann Marie proposed to Edda that they collaborate on a book of tours, opening Edda's fascinating "back street view" of Istanbul to visitors from around the world.

So—here it is. Your window into Edda's Istanbul—Stamboul's past.

Edda Renker Weissenbacher's Istanbul

Edda Weissenbacher (maiden name Renker) is Turkish born and married to an Austrian—a world citizen with a passion for Istanbul. I first encountered Edda while teaching high school in Istanbul when a friend invited me to join one of her informal walking tours of the hans.

Though I had found the standard tours of Sultanahmet awe-inspiring, a walk with Edda injected me with the wealth of history evoked on nearly every street in Sultanahmet. She revealed the magic of its hans (ancient inns) and bazaars, encouraging me to imagine the daily life of the denizens of eras past.

Edda opened my eyes, and Istanbul captured my heart.

Born in Istanbul in 1938, Edda spoke German at home with her parents. Her father was born in Vienna and emigrated to Istanbul as a child. (Edda was named after her Austrian grandmother.) Edda had a French nanny, and grew up in a Greek neighborhood, so she spoke German, French, and Greek as a child. She learned Turkish in elementary school, then English at the English High School for Girls in Beyoğlu, then studied French at Notre Dame de Sion in Harbiye. After working as a translator/secretary for a few years, she married and moved to Switzerland, where her son and daughter were born. Both her children were premature, so she took special care to create educational games to help them catch up with their peers. This time spent as a home educator became habitual with her, and she enjoyed playfully introducing her children to the cultural elements of their world.

When Edda returned to Istanbul in 1966, she discovered that her beloved city was rapidly changing. Her love for Istanbul drew her out of the house when her children grew up and left home; she spent countless hours wandering the streets of the city, chatting with artisans and shopkeepers. "The more I found out," she said, "the more fascinated I became, and I began to share my discoveries with friends and the friends of friends. It became a passion to find out more. As they say, hunger for knowledge is the best university."

Edda published a small photographic guide to the Kariye (Chora Church) Museum and another book on İznik tiles, leading her readers to some of the least expected quarters of Istanbul (both in multiple languages). Having been raised in a multicultural society and being married to an Austrian, Edda's friends and acquaintances came from many different communities and countries.

I convinced Edda that her gold mine of information needed to be shared; everyone should be able to experience her unique perspective of Old Istanbul. Combining Edda's historical expertise with my writing and photographs, we embarked on this project. If you can't take a walk with Edda, this guide is surely the next best thing.

What is a Han?

You may have noticed that many commercial buildings in the older sections of Istanbul are called hans. There's good reason for this. During the Middle Ages and the Renaissance, particularly during the Seljuk and Ottoman eras, caravansaries were built along trade routes between cities where travelers, often merchants, could spend a few nights. Within city walls one would find the same thing on a smaller scale, called a han (inn). The word "*han*" means house in Persian. The oldest existing han in Istanbul is the Balkapanı Han (walk D), which was built between the 4th and 5th centuries, during the Byzantine era. Most of the hans were constructed during the Ottoman Empire and the majority of those still standing date back to the 18th century.

Hans within the city consisted of an open porticoed courtyard surrounded by two or three stories of rooms, usually built of heavy stone or a combination of stone and brick. The windowless ground-floor rooms were used either to store goods that had been transported for sale or as stables. Upper-story rooms were shared by four to six people. Each evening they laid their mattresses on the floor of their rooms and in the morning rolled them up and stashed them into alcoves or cupboards to make space for daytime activity. While some rooms were used for sleeping, others were dedicated to working at a trade. Each of these rooms had a fireplace, as stone buildings (and Istanbul winters) can be very cold. Many of the old hans still have small domes and chimneys, each belonging to a cell. Many people spent their days distributing merchandise or selling it on the streets or in the bazaar.

The horses and camels of traveling merchants were sometimes stabled in ground-floor rooms, but the stables were usually located underground in basements, some of which had served as cisterns at one time. Animals walked down a stone ramp that usually sloped down from a second courtyard.

Nearly every han had a fountain in the courtyard and a kitchen in the building. Many also had a small mosque or a prayer room for the convenience of those residing there. Some hans housed different populations, perhaps Persians or Jews, so their places of worship reflected the specific population of each han. (For instance, the small synagogue in the Çorapçı Han was installed upstairs during the 20th century, nearly 400 years after the han was built.) Of course, the majority of the mosques were Sunni Muslim, as that was the preferred denomination of the Ottomans, as it is of most Turks today.

Hans had huge entries, usually large enough for camel or horse caravans to enter without dismounting. The entry was secured by massive iron-clad wooden gates that were locked and barred every evening to be reopened in the morning. These protected them not only from burglars but also from the many fires of that era. Many of the larger hans had a second gate leading to another street. People felt safe inside the han and welcomed the opportunity to socialize and make friends in the courtyard and galleries.

Hans were usually named after the merchandise that was sold there: Zincirli (chains) Han, Kundakçı (wooden part of a gun) Han, Cebeci (armor) Han, Sepetçi (baskets) Han, Astarcı (lining) Han, Çorapçı (stocking) Han, Sabuncu (soap) Han, etc. (Language note: the -çi, -ci, -çı, -cı, -çu, -cu ending means "the one who makes or sells.")

As transportation and commerce became more sophisticated at the end of the 19th century, merchants no longer traveled in caravans. Populations became more stable and less nomadic, hence there was little need for hans

to be used as inns. The stables of the old hans were transformed into warehouses, while upstairs rooms became primarily workshop facilities, with each han dedicated to a specific trade (weaving, goldsmithing, etc.).

Many hans still serve as workshops to this day, although most have been taken over by wholesale and retail merchants. Hans built after the 19th century look more like office and retail buildings than the historical hans organized around a courtyard.

As you wander the city, note the names written above the main entrances of buildings. You may be surprised to discover how very many of the buildings in Old Istanbul bear the name han. The word "han" has come to mean a building where there are offices or workshops, with very few used as housing.

Although today these ancient hans have become commercial buildings rather than inns, it's fascinating to explore them, gazing at their crumbling walls and ornate Ottoman fountains to imagine the teeming activity that filled them for centuries. These hans are your window to the captivating legacy of Old Istanbul.

Mosques: A Window to Islamic Life

Today we celebrate mosques for their architectural beauty and as a place of worship and prayer. Recited five times daily, the call to prayer is an integral part of the lives of Muslims, while for many of the rest of us it is a treasured reminder of the essence of Turkish culture. Though over 99 percent of the Turkish population is Muslim, many are not active worshippers. Most Turkish Muslims are Sunni.

Many people don't realize that the Muslim faith follows the teachings of both the *Old Testament* and the *New Testament*, although Muslims see Jesus as a prophet rather than as their savior. The core of the religion is found in the *Quran*, the sacred book of Islam, which Muslims believe to be the word of God as revealed to the Prophet Mohammed.

In Ottoman times, the mosque served a greater role in the lives of citizens. Usually financed by a sultan, his mother, or a grand vizier (sultan's chief advisor), mosques were intended to extol Allah, to stand as a permanent tribute to the founder (and pave his way to heaven), and to serve the religious needs of the public. In addition, a *külliye* was often built

around the mosque. A *külliye* was a complex of buildings that served the physical and intellectual needs of the public. *Külliyes* often included soup kitchens, hospitals, fountains, water distribution kiosks (*sebils*), schools (*medreses*), bathhouses (*hamams*), and inns (*hans*). They often included bazaars as well; these helped to financially support the services of the *külliye*. Few mosque *külliyes* remain, though some of the original buildings still stand. Of the mosques in this book, Beyazıt (walk A) and Süleymaniye (walk D) boast the most extensive intact *külliye* complexes.

For centuries the call to prayer was made from the balcony (*şerefe*) of a minaret by a *müezzin*. Today the call to prayer is broadcast through loudspeakers by the *müezzin,* who chants comfortably from inside the mosque. If you are lucky, you may see a *müezzin* standing on the *şerefe* of a small mosque, his hands cupped behind his ears or around his mouth.

It is truly exhilarating to be outdoors in Istanbul when the call to prayer fills the air from scores of minarets. There's certainly no point in continuing conversation until the prayer ends, and it never hurts to ponder your own spirituality as you listen.

Before Muslims enter a mosque to pray, they must perform ablutions, or washing of the feet, hands, and face at fountains outside the mosque. Usually women wash at fountains separate from those used by men; there are more discrete indoor faucets available for more private ablutions. Those at prayer always face Mecca as they lower their heads in humility and respect for Allah.

When you enter a mosque it is important to observe the religious rituals. Women should have their heads covered (female tourists should always carry a scarf), men should remove their hats, and both men and women should remove their shoes before entering. Shoulders and knees should also be covered, although some mosques are more diligent at enforcing this than others. Avoid taking photos with a flash and stay discreetly behind those who are at prayer. Few mosques require a donation but there is always a donation box available, and of course your support is always appreciated.

The raised platform in large mosques is called the *müezzin mahfili.* It is where the *müezzin* stands to chant responses to the prayers of the *imam* (prayer leader).

The ornate niche in the wall which marks the direction to Mecca is called the *mihrap.* You will note that those who pray tend to focus on that spot.

The tall pulpit with stairs to the top is called the *minber.* This is where the *imam* delivers the sermon at midday on Friday as well as on religious holidays. Visitors are asked to stay outside the mosque during the prayer services, the exact times of which change daily according to sunrise and sunset.

Using This Guide

These four walks are designed to introduce you to some of the lesser-known yet fascinating sites of Old Istanbul. The walks were originally designed around the city's old hans (inns), but they include other ancient edifices along the routes as well. While you walk, take time to gaze above the street-level storefronts, which often mask the age of the buildings.

Each of these walks can be completed in three to four hours (possibly raced through in an hour). If you're into marathons, you could even complete all four in a day—which would be CRAZY! We recommend taking your time to thoroughly explore one walk at a time. Each walk continues from the last site of the previous walk, which we hoped would simplify getting your bearings. This area may seem daunting at first, so we've done our best to design clear maps and directions to guide you through your adventure into Old Istanbul.

Consider yourself an intrepid explorer—an anthropologist on assignment. The magic of Turkey is found in its fascinating history and its warm, welcoming people. Take time to enjoy both as you follow these routes: engage shopkeepers and artisans in conversation, accept the occasional proffered drink, and keep your eyes open to wonder at every little detail. The more time you take, the more you'll learn. As you walk, though, be sure to secure your wallet, as pickpockets are common in most tourist areas, especially the crowded streets and bazaars.

Directions from site to site are in beige boxes, and foreign words are italicized. We've attempted to create simple phonetic pronunciations for each of the sites. Introductory pieces will also give you general background on hans and mosques, as well as offering a historical timeline to help you place things in perspective. In the back of the book you'll find a glossary of commonly used Turkish terms as well as a chart of information on the Ottoman sultans.

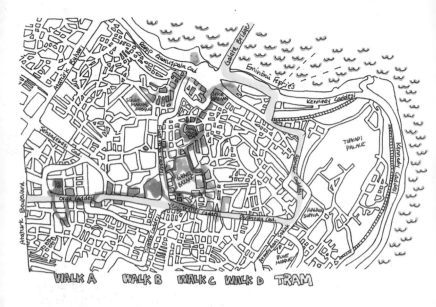

WALK A
West of the Grand Bazaar: Taş Han to Fuat Ali Paşa Mosque
6 hans, 4 mosques/churches, 3 *medreses* (Muslim theological institutes), and other sites

WALK B
In and around the Grand Bazaar: Fuat Ali Paşa Mosque to Zincirli Han
14 hans, 4 mosques/churches, and other sites

WALK C
Behind the Grand Bazaar: Zincirli Han to the Spice Bazaar
20 hans, 2 mosques, and other sites

WALK D
Hans above Eminönü: Spice Bazaar to Zindan Han
12 hans, 6 mosques, and other sites

General Tips for the Walks

- Be sure to wear sturdy, comfortable shoes. You'll be walking on cobbled streets, which are a challenge in any event.
- Women should have a scarf along for visits to mosques. Some provide scarves but many don't. Please don't enter a mosque if you're scantily dressed.
- There are few street signs in Istanbul, so you need to look for small square blue signs posted at the upper corner of some shop doorways along the street. The bottom name on the plate is the name of the street you're on.
- If you get confused, be sure to ask for help. Shopkeepers are generally very helpful and most passersby will be happy to give you a hand. Of course, many Turks are so kind that if they don't know the right answer, they'll give you any answer they think might please you.
- Touts may badger you to come into their shops and buy. A simple refusal to this harassment is "*İstemiyorum, sağ ol.*" [iss-STEM-mee-OR-um, SOWL] This means, "I don't want anything, thanks." Say it kindly but firmly. You can also say "*hayır,*" a little like "higher," which means "no" but is less polite. A "stop" motion with your hand communicates your message as well.
- The bazaar areas and the streets between them are particularly crowded on Saturdays, so try to avoid doing these walks on those days. Early in the day things are quieter, too. Remember that on Sundays the Grand Bazaar, the Spice Bazaar, and the hans are closed. The streets are quieter, but you'll miss a lot of the highlights.
- We've included WC alerts for clean restrooms along the way, but you need to plan a bit. Most public restrooms that require a fee are kept quite clean. You may need to learn to use a "stooper" (squat toilet), but usually there is a Western toilet available. Be sure to have tissues with you, just in case there's no paper.

A historical engraving of the Laleli Mosque.

Walk A
West of the Grand Bazaar

TO BEGIN WALK A:

From the Laleli tram stop at the intersection of Ordu Caddesi (the tramline) and Büyük Reşit Paşa Caddesi, cross to the huge concrete University Faculty building with the gold silhouette of Atatürk decorating the second story above the entrance. Cross Büyük Reşit Paşa Caddesi and walk two blocks along the tramline to Fethi Bey Caddesi. You will have just passed a gold, block-long hotel building, the Crowne Plaza Hotel. Turn right after the hotel and walk up two blocks, one block beyond the hotel complex. On the left side of the street you will see the old arched entrance to your first han.

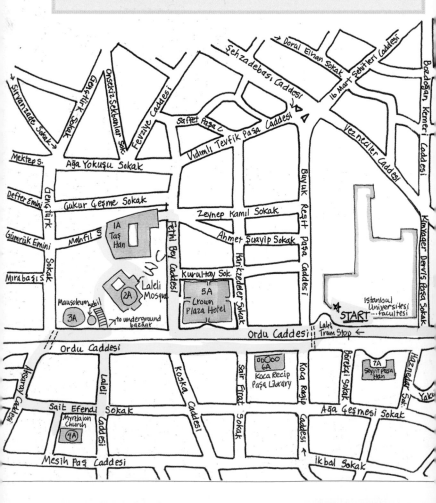

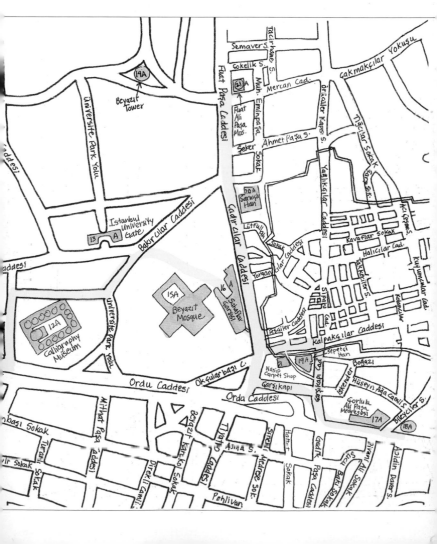

TAŞ HAN–1A
[TAHSH hahn]

Since its recent restoration, the Taş Han looks much the same as it did over two hundred years ago, making it an excellent example for your first view of a han. It was constructed in 1763 over an ancient Byzantine cistern as a part of the Laleli Mosque complex, commissioned by Sultan Mustafa III. Designed by the ingenious baroque architect Mehmet Tahir Ağa, it was initially built as an inn for travelers, particularly army horsemen (known in Turkish as *sipahi*) when they came from the provinces once a month to get their pay. This is why it was originally called Sipahi Han. When the *sipahi* no longer came here, the han was used mainly for merchant travelers. Its name was changed to Çukur Çeşme Han, which means "sunken fountain," because of a sunken fountain that existed around the corner. (Each time a

Hans were small caravansaries or inns within the city walls, usually around the bazaar area, where travelers and merchants could spend a few nights. They generally consisted of two stories of rooms arranged around a porticoed courtyard. Often the lower rooms were used as warehouses for storing merchandise until the merchants moved on, while the upper-story rooms were used as lodgings. Most hans had a fountain and a kitchen, and some had a mescit (small mosque) in the courtyard. (For more information on hans, see the introduction to this guide.)

street is paved, it rises by a few centimeters, so over the years many of the city's fountains have appeared "sunken" in comparison to the current street level.) After the founding of the Turkish Republic this han was given the

unassuming name Taş Han ("stone building").

Back to the Taş Han today: The main entrance leads through a vaulted passage lined with shops and archways, ending at an open porticoed courtyard also surrounded by numerous shops.

Walk up the stone stairway on your left at the end of the first corridor (before the open courtyard) for the best view of the han's courtyard.

Istanbulites sip tea as they play backgammon (*tavla*).

At the far end of the courtyard you'll see stairs leading down to what was probably a cistern during the Byzantine period, then a stable during Ottoman times. Many of the surrounding shops—originally storage rooms for merchandise belonging to travelers—are irregularly shaped, probably an indication of the creative independence of the han's designer. Beyond the courtyard are passages to two additional courtyards, one of which has been turned into a restaurant.

The crumbling Taş Han was rescued by Kemal Ocak, who oversaw its meticulous restoration from 1993-1996. Though this restoration was financed privately (by his family), it was endorsed by the Turkish Department of Antiquities. The han now houses numerous clothing shops, and plans are in progress to convert much of it to a hotel. The han has a teahouse in the courtyard as well as two excellent restaurants, the Taşhan Restaurant on the ground floor and the elegant Arkat Restaurant/Night Club in the underground cistern. Take time to peek into the Arkat to get a sense of the stables of yesteryear (if it's closed, ask someone to help you find a manager to open it), then ramble through the courtyards to experience the full effect of this impressive restoration.

➡ " See profile of founder Kemal Ocak on page 58-59."

Across the courtyard on the ground floor is a hallway where you'll find the Taşhan Restaurant with its lovely open courtyard. This corridor leads outside to Mahfil Sokak. Take an immediate left outside the door and follow the narrow passageway along the building, up some stairs, and then to your right through an entrance to the Laleli Mosque courtyard. As you pass through the archway, turn around to see a small birdhouse between the upper windows of the Taş Han. This is the first of many you will see on buildings from the Ottoman era.

LALELİ CAMİSİ (MOSQUE)—2A
[LAH-lay-lee JAH-mee-see]

Laleli Mosque (Tulip Mosque) built from 1759–1763, is thought to be the finest of Istanbul's baroque mosques. Financed by Sultan Mustafa III, it was designed by Mehmet Tahir Ağa, one of the Ottoman Empire's most unconventional architects. Some find his style charming while others find it a bit ostentatious. Whatever your reactions, it's an interesting building. The minarets do not have the usual conical lead roof but are designed to look like tulip bulbs. The tulip—*lale* in Turkish—is a symbol of Istanbul.

On the mosque's second level, a long ramp runs up the east side of the building, leading to the Imperial Loge, the private prayer space reserved for the sultan. It was designed so that the sultan could ride horseback directly to his loge. (Whether this was for convenience, privacy, or sheer laziness is uncertain. You probably know that many sultans were well portioned, to put it nicely.) Note the Ottoman script over the sultan's entrance at the bottom of the ramp.

Walk around the mosque to your right, which will lead you to the main entrance, as well as the soup kitchen beyond the mosque.

The walls of the mosque are made of layers of brick and stones, as was the Taş Han. The Ottomans learned this technique from the

Byzantines, who built the city's walls in the fourth century. They discovered that bricks are more shock-absorbent and softer than stone, so walls made with alternate layers of both materials combine the strength of stone with the flexibility of brick, making them less apt to crumble when shaken during an earthquake.

The interior of the Tulip Mosque is rectangular in shape with eight semidomes forming an octagon above it, and its multicolored marble décor, though fascinating, borders on being gaudy. It's clear, though, that a creative mind combined stone (both marble and semiprecious stones), wood, and mother-of-pearl with great finesse. Note the sultan's gold-screened loge on the upper level. These loges only appear in mosques built by sultans.

The elaborate *müezzin mahfili* in the Laleli Mosque.

Beyond the mosque on your right is another building, which served as a soup kitchen for many years. Turn left and walk down the stairway along the wall.

Halfway down on your right you'll see an Ottoman fountain (the spigots are gone), a clear example of the ornate baroque style of this mosque complex.

Take a left into the passage at the bottom of the stairs before the sidewalk; it will lead you to a gallery of shops under the mosque.

WC ALERT: There is a very clean restroom to the left inside the entry to this market.

Mosques were usually commissioned by sultans or other persons of high station. If the person was someone from the imperial family, the mosque could have more than one minaret. Often they included a külliye, a complex of buildings to serve the public. These may have included a *medrese* (school), a soup kitchen, a hospital, a han (inn), a *hamam* (bathhouse), and sometimes a bazaar to raise funds to support the mosque and its charitable foundations. (For more information, refer to the introduction to this book.)

Top photo: The Laleli Soup Kitchen.
Lower photo: A young man performs ablutions before prayer.

Amazingly, the entire mosque sits on a huge slab supported by eight enormous piers, more evidence of the genius of Mehmet Tahir Ağa. Take a moment to rest in this hall where they once cooled drinks in a central white marble fountain. (Unfortunately, the fountain is most likely filled with merchandise today.) Envision this spot two hundred years ago, awash with robed merchants and citizens going about their daily errands in the bazaar. Throughout the centuries, these shops have generated funds to support the Laleli Mosque complex.

Step back outside to the bottom of the stairway and turn right onto the street to see an ancient *sebil* and tomb.

SEBİL & MAUSOLEUM OF SULTAN MUSTAFA III–3A
[say-BILL, moo-stah-FAH]

The first building you see here is a *sebil*. During Ottoman times it was considered a good deed to provide people with water, so many pious people had fountains built in their names. Those who could afford it built an additional *sebil* ("path" in Persian) like this one for distributing drinks. Mosque attendants would hand out water, tea, and lemonade through its ornate convex grilles to thirsty passersby. The person paying for the service was, of course, paving himself a "path" to heaven.

Notice the baroque carving on the underside of the eaves of this *sebil*.

Step beyond the sebil to a two-story octagonal building nearer to the corner.

This is the Mausoleum of Sultan Mustafa III and his son Sultan Selim III, who was murdered in 1808 by palace officials. Look carefully above the windows and you'll see small birdhouses built into the stonework under the eaves. The Ottomans believed birds to be semi-sacred as they considered them halfway between earth and heaven. They often built little birdhouses to accommodate them, again "paving" their way to heaven.

Walk to the corner beyond the tomb and cross Ordu Caddesi. You'll jog a bit to the right; then turn left and follow Aksaray Caddesi until you see a marble stairway leading up to your left. Walk up the stairs and you'll come onto a huge open courtyard. Beyond the courtyard you'll see the lovely Myrelaion Church, now Bodrum Camisi.

MYRELAION CHURCH (BODRUM CAMİSİ)–4A
(The Church of the Holy Anointing Oil)
[mee-RAY-lah-yohn]

You are now standing on an open terrace over a Roman rotunda, or circular building, begun in the fifth century. It measured 30 meters in diameter on the inside, nearly as large as the Pantheon in Rome; imagine what a different place this was sixteen centuries ago. Unfortunately, it remained unfinished for five hundred years. During the 10th century, Emperor Romanus I Lecapenus added 75 columns to support a roof and used it as a cistern. He had a small palace constructed on top of it, then had this church built nearby to serve the residents of the palace. After the 15th century it was no longer used as a cistern but as a warehouse and dump.

The very lovely Myrelaion Church was constructed over a tall basement, which raised it to the level of the palace. (The basement was later used as a crypt.) It is a four-column church topped not with a dome but with a drum and rounded corners, a style popular at that time. You can see a few similarly built churches in Istanbul, including the famous Chora Church near the outer city walls.

The church's name, Greek for "oil of myrrh," is the same as that of a nearby monastery whose nuns were driven out during the period of iconoclasm in the eighth

Ancient engraving of the Bodrum Mosque.

century (iconoclasts were opposed to religious icons). Iconoclasm began in 730, when Emperor Leo III ordered the destruction of all figurative representations. It was most likely a political move to unify the church throughout the Byzantine Empire and possibly to improve the morality of his subjects. It has also been suggested that one of his motives was to make the churches less dazzling in order to attract more young men to the military rather than the clergy. Whatever Leo's motive, many iconodules (people in favor of icons) wanted sacred images restored to churches, monasteries and homes. Nearly a century later, in 843, Emperor Michael III declared the restoration of icons. Of course, that happened before this church was built, but it sheds an interesting light on the religious fervor of the era. (Remember, too, that at that time Muslim influence was growing in this area and Islam forbids the display of human images.)

Mesih Ali Paşa converted the church to a mosque in the late 15th century. It is now known as Bodrum Camisi, which means "mosque with a cellar." The tombs found in the crypt were transferred to the Istanbul Archaeological Museum.

Continue across the courtyard along Sait Efendi Sokak to Laleli Caddesi and turn left, walking one block to Ordu Caddesi. (You will see Laleli Mosque up the street.) Take a right on Ordu Caddesi and follow it along the tramline east toward Sultanahmet. The ornate buildings across the street on your left after you pass Laleli Mosque are the Crowne Plaza Hotel.

CROWNE PLAZA HOTEL–5A
(Merit Antique Hotel)

open courtyard where the residents' children loved to play. Probably because of their appealing design, the streets and courtyards were eventually covered over and converted into a hotel—first the Ramada, then the Merit Antique Hotel. It has recently undergone further extensive renovation to become the current Crowne Plaza Hotel.

These identical four blocks of buildings were constructed in 1918 as government-sponsored flats for civil servants and their families. The buildings have a European flavor, popular in Istanbul after the turn of the century. Each building had many small flats arranged around an

As you continue along Ordu Caddesi, on your right (the south side of the street) you will see an ancient building with domes and a central arched entrance that has gold Arabic writing above the door.

LIBRARY OF KOCA RAGIP PAŞA–6A
[koh-JAH rah-GUHP pah-SHAH]

Koca Ragıp was Sultan Mustafa III's Grand Vizier for six years. According to Istanbul historian John Freely, Ragıp Pasa "is considered to have been the last of the great men to hold that office. [He] was also the best poet of his time and composed some of the most apt and witty of the chronograms inscribed on the street-fountains of Istanbul." (*Strolling Through Istanbul*, 193).

Ragıp Paşa had this *medrese* built in 1752. It was most likely designed by Mehmet Tahir Ağa, who designed the entire Laleli complex. Above the gate there was the *mektep* (primary school), recently used as a children's library. The domed lobby to the left of the main building was used as a private prayer room. A niche shows the direction of Mecca and there is a picture of Ragıp Paşa beside it. The square reading room of the main library, which had actually been the main classroom of the original *medrese*, has a central dome supported by four columns. Manuscripts are held in a "cage" of bronze grilles between the columns.

The lovely blue and white tiles on the walls were brought from Italy and the cupboard doors are marquetry (made of inlaid wood). Oil lamps once hung from the ceiling's wooden calligraphic decorations, reminding one of Chinese lanterns. This is a lovely spot to just sit and enjoy the peace and quiet of an ancient *medrese*.

Unfortunately, this building was damaged in the 1999 earthquake and was consequently closed to the public. If you are lucky, perhaps renovations will have been completed and you'll be able to tour this charming complex, which was converted to a library in the early 1900s.

April 2017 - still not open

Cross Ordu Caddesi at the crosswalk beyond the Koca Ragıp Paşa Library. (This is the Laleli tram stop where you began this walk.) Turn right and follow Ordu Caddesi two more blocks, toward Beyazıt and you will see a partially destroyed han on the opposite (south) side of the street.

SEYYİT HASAN PAŞA HAN–7A
[say-EET hah-SAHN pah-SHAH]

This han was constructed around 1740 specifically for VIPs, funded by Grand Vizier Seyyit Hasan Paşa. Since it did not house merchants, there was no need for stables or storerooms like most hans. Instead, it had elegant multi-room suites, several marble columns, and two lovely rococo fountains.

Unfortunately, part of the han was demolished when the street was widened, and it has clearly lost its past luster. Today brooms are sold here, so it is called Süpürgeciler Hanı (broom sellers' han). There are of course other types of merchandise sold here as well.

Look to your left on your side of the street (north), and you will see a huge, square, domed building with a stairway leading up on its left.

BEYAZIT HAMAMI–8A
[bay-ah-ZUHT ha-mah-MUH]

This building is the most westerly of the Beyazıt complex. The Beyazıt Hamamı was built in 1500 and was once one of Istanbul's most opulent public baths. (Unlike Europeans, who then bathed only once or twice a year, the Ottomans believed in cleanliness of both heart and body, so *hamams* were important in their lives.) The *hamam*'s two domes remind us that one section was for women and the other for men, with the women's section somewhat smaller and less ornate. The men's and women's sections had entrances on different façades, as was the tradition of the time.

This grand *hamam* suffered a serious crack in its western wall from the 1999 earthquake, after which major renovations and restorations were done. Behind the two main domes are many smaller domes and vaults, now completely restored. The two large domes covered the *hamam*'s *soğukluk* (cooling room), while the smaller anterior domes covered the *hararet* (heating area), where lovely marble sinks were arranged around a heated marble slab (to lie on and to enjoy soap massages). Some fragments from the Forum of Theodosius across the street were used in the original foundation of the *hamam*; see if you can

Beyazıt Hamamı before restoration.

Bather in a *hamam* (right),
hamam sandals (*takunya*) (above).

discover them as you walk to the
next site.

An interesting historical note
about this *hamam* is that the 1730
Rebellion of Patrona Halil ended
in bloodshed here after a mob
uprising that replaced Sultan
Ahmet III with Mahmud I. The
revolt was led by a *hamam* attendant,
Patrona Halil, who fled into
the *hamam* with his followers to
escape the sultan's soldiers. Halil
survived the attack, but was assassinated
six years later.

Walk up the stairway
beside the *hamam*, noting
the many domes in the
back part of the building.
Look ahead beyond the open
courtyard to see another
ancient building behind the
hamam.

SEYYİT HASAN PAŞA MEDRESESİ–9A
[say-EET hah-SAHN pah-SHAH may-dray-say-see]

Seyyit Hasan Paşa Medresesi (above) and close-up of birdhouse beneath the south eaves (below).

Up the steps from the Beyazıt Hamamı is the Seyyit Hasan Paşa Medresesi, which has Istanbul's loveliest Ottoman birdhouse nestled beneath its south eaves. Fashioned after a mosque, it has tiny minarets in relief on each side. (As was noted earlier in the Laleli complex description, the Ottomans often incorporated stone birdhouses on the façades of their structures as their way of "feathering their flight" to heav-

en.) You will see unmistakable signs that this miniature edifice continues to be used by many birds.

Go back down the stairway, remembering to look for remnants of the Forum of Theodosius at the base of the *hamam* as you pass. Along the sidewalk on both sides of the street you'll see huge fragments of marble columns and pediments from that ancient forum.

FORUM OF THEODOSIUS–10A
[THEE-o-DOH-see-us]

Column fragments along Ordu Caddesi.

Beyazıt Square (further to the east) was once Constantinople's largest public square. It was built by Byzantine Emperor Theodosius I (the Great) in A.D. 393 on the site of a colossal Roman bronze statue of a bull. This ancient Forum Tauri (Bull Forum) was constructed to commemorate victorious Roman soldiers, whose bas-reliefs adorned the marble columns of the forum. The bodies of criminals were burned beside this statue.

Fragments from the forum's columns were used in the construction of the Beyazıt Hamamı as well as many other structures in the area. Looking along the street, one can still see parts of the gigantic triumphal arch (one pediment remains intact on the south side of the street), Corinthian capitals, and columns with reliefs of peacock-feather eyes (thought by some historians to be upside-down tears). What a contrast to see these ancient pediments used to display suitcases and clothing for shoppers—it's the sign of the times.

Walk further up the street and look for a small open area beyond some ancient marble foundations in the sidewalk. Take a left up a stairway that leads to a small parking lot. Look behind you for a good view of the lovely restored han across the street just behind the ruins of the Forum of Theodosius.

SİMKEŞHANE–11A
[seem-KESH-hahn-NAY]

Fatih Sultan Mehmet II (Mehmet the Conqueror) was the sultan who conquered Constantinople, although he was actually the seventh Ottoman sultan. He destroyed a monastery that stood on this site, scattering the deposed alchemist monks. He then built an imperial mint here as well as a wooden palace on the other side of the forum, where Istanbul University now stands. (How ironic that alchemy—the science of formulating gold—was ousted and replaced by the minting of coins.) The sultan seldom resided at this palace, however, as the Ottoman capital was still Edirne.

A decade or so later, Mehmet II moved the capital to Istanbul and began construction on Topkapı Palace, to which succeeding sultans added more buildings.

The mint, which produced both gold and silver coins, was eventually transferred to the new palace and this building was renovated in the 18th century for use by spinners of gold and silver thread.

Most likely you have seen and admired the Ottoman caftans made of silk or velvet embroidered with gold and silver thread; the thread was produced here. *Sim* means gold or silver thread; *keş* is a suffix, meaning one who spins it; and *han* or *hane* is a building, hence Simkeşhane. Unfortunately, thread is no longer produced here; this lovely building has been recently restored and is now used as a library.

WC ALERT: There's a very clean restroom midway up the stairway you're standing on.

> The stairs will lead you to Beyazıt Square, a huge plaza surrounded by Beyazıt Mosque, Beyazıt Medresesi, and the Istanbul University Gate. As you enter the square, the smaller multi-domed structure on your right (the west side of the square) is the medrese.

CALLIGRAPHY MUSEUM–12A
(HAT MÜZESİ, formerly BEYAZIT MEDRESESİ)
[HAHT mew-zay-SEE, bay-ah-ZUHT may-dray-say-see]

The Medrese

*Medrese*s were theological schools and early universities where boys and young men were taught a variety of subjects including law, science, and medicine. Each dome and chimney of this ancient *medrese* represents one of the many cells arranged around the charming porticoed courtyard. Four to six students shared each of the cells, which were entered through small doors leading from the gallery. They rolled simple mattresses out to sleep at night and stored them away in cupboards each morning.

Boys studied in a central lecture room at the far end of the courtyard. They had no benches or tables, so they sat cross-legged on the floor, which was covered with straw mats. As soon as the *müezzin* called from nearby Beyazıt Mosque, they set aside their books, transforming the lecture hall into a prayer room. They washed their faces, hands, and feet at the courtyard's ablution

fountain, then returned to pray facing the niche (*mihrap*), which was directed toward Mecca and adorned with the name of God (Allah) and that of the Prophet (Muhammed).

This former classroom now houses numerous sacred relics: a hair from the Prophet's beard, soil from the holy city of Mecca, and the lovely Kaaba curtain embroidered with gold and silver thread spun in the Simkeşhane. It was the custom for the sultan to send a new Kaaba curtain to Mecca every year to cover the holy Black Stone. The old curtain was then cut into pieces and given to deserving dignitaries. This room is usually closed, opening only during the month of *Ramazan* (Ramadan) for pilgrims to come and meditate.

Ottoman calligraphy in gold on black.

After Atatürk established the Republic in 1923, he had the *medrese*s in Turkey closed so that all children, including girls, could attend public schools and learn to read and write the modernized Turkish language. (The Ottoman language and alphabet were abandoned at that time.) The *medrese*s were no longer looked after properly and many fell into disrepair. Fortunately, this particular *medrese* was renovated and is now used as a calligraphy museum (closed on Sundays and Mondays). The hand-painted designs on the exterior of the building above the door are original.

The Museum

Islam forbids the representation of human beings in pictures, since man was created in the likeness of God. While women embroidered, men occupied themselves with decorative writing. Calligraphy is said to be three arts in one: it is so beautiful that it can be hung on the wall like a picture; it has a meaning (if you can read Ottoman or Arabic); and if the person who reads it aloud has a nice voice, it sounds musical.

The calligraphy in this museum is all in the Ottoman language, which resembles Arabic much more than it does modern Turkish. Ottoman contained elements of three languages: Persian, Arabic, and Turkish (part of the Ural-Altaic language family, which includes Hungarian, Estonian, Finnish, etc.).

Ottoman is written from right to left using the Arabic alphabet; the graceful lines go upward towards heaven and look like *kayık*s, those slim gondola-like boats that were used long ago to cross the Bosphorus. Most of the framed calligraphies hanging on

Medrese domes as viewed from inner courtyard.

the walls are made up of harmonious loops attached to one another, which are consonants. The vowels are the small signs arranged around them; these can be omitted because words can be deciphered without them. But the vowels clarify meaning and also add to the beauty of these pieces. Almost all the calligraphy in this museum has been done with rounded letters, a style called *sülüs* that started in the 18th century. The straight-lined style with right angles at the corners, *kûfî*, predominated before that time.

The sultans' decrees (*firman*s) were written out by calligraphers, many of whom were dervishes, as the "dervish-hat" signature indicates. (Using their own signatures would have been an insult to the sultan.)

The *tuğra* was the sovereign's symbol, which he chose from several that were shown to him when he acceded to the throne. He used the same one throughout his reign. All *tuğra*s look similar but include different words, like the sultan's name and his honorific titles. The more important a sultan was, the lower the text started on the page, which left more space for his signature. Leaves and flowers decorated the space between the lines and the whole piece was beautifully framed with intricate floral

Illuminated manuscript of the Koran.

made up of miniscule letters—the entire Quran is written on this single sheet of paper! The calligrapher devoted seven years to this amazing piece, which was completed in 1887.

The museum also has examples of marbleized paper, called *ebru*, or "cloud" in Persian. (It is quite similar to the oil type of Easter egg decorating.) *Ebru* is

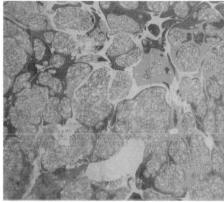

Example of *ebru*, payer marbling.

ornamentation. Some sultans were calligraphers themselves and enjoyed writing in their own free time.

The museum includes many unique examples of calligraphy. Look for the delicate calligraphy drawn on dried leaves, calligraphy cut from paper, and calligraphy embroidered on and woven into cloth. There is also a perpetual seven-year Islamic calendar, as well as a document with each letter formed by a paragraph of tiny calligraphic print. There is also a clear bottle with calligraphy in both yellow and black; the yellow has been written on the outside of the bottle, while the black is on the inside.

In the southeast corner of the museum is an ornate, abstract representation of a *Bektaşi* (member of a dervish order) sitting cross-legged. If you look at it very closely, you will see that it is

created by spreading different colors onto a thick liquid. When a sheet of paper is placed on the surface to absorb the ink, the colors move, making each specimen unique. As you probably know, *ebru* has been used mainly for binding books and matting pictures.

As you exit the Museum of Calligraphic Art, cross the square, looking to your left at the huge gate on the north side of the square.

ISTANBUL UNIVERSITY GATE–13A

Although this university was probably in existence from the time of the Ottoman conquest in 1453, possibly as a part of the *medrese*, this elaborate gate was built in 1866 by the French architect Auguste Bourgeois. He also designed the nondescript main building nearby that once housed the Ministry of War. The university was originally established for the study of religion and philosophy, although it eventually expanded to law, medicine, and science—in spite of significant resistance to westernization of the curriculum by the *ulema*, the religious hierarchy of the Ottoman Empire.

The main buildings of Istanbul University stand on the site of Sultan Mehmet the Conqueror's original wooden palace, the Eski Saray or Old Seraglio (*eski* means old and *saray* means palace). After the sultans moved to Topkapı Palace, the Eski Saray was used to house the harems and female relatives of former sultans. As you experience the never-ending bustle of Beyazıt Square, try to imagine this huge area surrounded by a mosque, several *medrese*s and a palace.

> Standing before the university gate, look beyond it to the right and you'll see a tall white tower, shaped something like a knife handle. Though you cannot enter the university grounds, you can see this tower from a number of vantage points in the area.

BEYAZIT TOWER–14A
[BAY-ah-zuht]

Beyazıt Tower, sitting at the highest point of the old city, was originally a fire tower, built of wood. A patrol was always posted at the top and, as soon as he saw any sign of a fire, he would shout to a team of firemen below. They would then grab their pump and run barefoot to the site to extinguish the fire. A spark from a brazier could easily set fire to a wooden house and, unfortunately, a whole community could easily burn in one night. The tower eventually burned down and this one, constructed in 1826—of stone— was financed by Sultan Mahmut II.

The tower is 50 meters tall with a wooden staircase of 180 steps, and it has a commanding view of the entire city. Because of recent heightened security, it is not possible for the public to enter the university grounds, so you can only admire it from afar.

 Now turn to look at the large mosque on the south side of the square.

BEYAZIT CAMİSİ (MOSQUE)–15A
[BAY-ah-zuht JAH-mee-see]

Sultan Beyazıt II, the son of Sultan Mehmet the Conqueror, had to sell some of his father's works of art to finance the building of this mosque in 1501. It is the oldest imperial mosque with a dome, since that of his father was destroyed by an earthquake (though it was later rebuilt).

The outside of the mosque is not particularly impressive, although the minaret nearest the *medrese* is intricately decorated with geometric terra cotta designs. The entry courtyard is impressive, though, with three huge entrances and 24 small domes surrounding it. Stalactite moldings decorate the capitals, cornices, and niches of the courtyard and round carved semidome reliefs are a unique addition to the upper walls. An impressive entrance leads to the main mosque, which is a simplified version of the Hagia Sophia (pronounced Aya Sofia). Four huge rectangular piers support the main dome and the semidomes emanating from it.

Much of the charm of Beyazıt Mosque is the activity that surrounds it. Women sell birdseed for the pigeons in front of the mosque to students, shoppers, businessmen, and tourists who bustle past. On the northeast side (your left as you face the mosque) groups of men in skullcaps discuss the Quran or sit contemplatively with their prayer beads.

Men meeting outside the Beyazıt Mosque's east entrance.

Beyazıt Mosque as viewed from the courtyard.

Others hawk their wares, generally of a religious nature. Occasionally a speaker will stand beneath one of the massive trees to lecture others on matters religious or otherwise. Inside the mosque, theology students can be found reading aloud from the Quran as people of all walks of life remove their shoes to bow in prayer. It is acceptable for tourists to view the inside of a mosque unless there is a prayer service, but remember to be covered appropriately.

Outer north entrance to the Beyazıt Mosque.

The building to the east of the mosque included the *imaret* (soup kitchen) of the *külliye* and a caravanserai (inn). In 1882 Sultan Abdülhamit II had it converted to a library, now the State Library, which holds over 120,000 volumes and 7,000 manuscripts.

> Pass through the shaded courtyard on the east side of the mosque beyond the groups of men and enter the gate to the used book bazaar.

SAHAFLAR ÇARŞISI–16A
[sah-hahf-LAR chahr-shuh-SUH]

You have entered the book bazaar through the Gate of the Spoonmakers. The Byzantines called this place Khartoprateia. The word "kharti" means paper in Greek, so we know it was the paper and book center of Constantinople. Now it is a market for both new and secondhand books as well as souvenirs. One of the oldest markets in the city, over the years its business has changed from making and selling paper to producing turbans to metal engraving and finally back to selling books.

Bust of İbrahim Müteferrika.

The modern bust in the center is that of İbrahim Müteferrika, who installed a printing press with Arabic characters here. Its first book was printed in 1727, three centuries after Gutenberg's press was begun in Europe. The sultan's calligraphers were upset that this might mean the end of their trade, so they destroyed the press. Müteferrika, undaunted, brought in another press and continued with his printing business. To appease the calligraphers, the printing of religious books on a press was forbidden.

The gate at the far end of the market is an ancient stone portal, Hakkaklar Kapısı, the Gate of the Engravers. This gate leads to the Grand Bazaar.

➤ " See profile of Tuğra shopowners Recai and Mustafa Akyol on page 60."

➤ " See profile of börek seller Adem Usta on page 61."

> 🚶 Turn right and walk along Çadırcılar Caddesi past three entrances to the Grand Bazaar until you reach the main sidewalk along Ordu Caddesi. Turn left along the sidewalk and follow it east along the tramline a few blocks until you reach an arched doorway on your left leading through a small cemetery.

ÇORLULU ALİ PAŞA MEDRESESİ–17A
[CHOHR-loo-loo ah-LEE pah-SHAH may-dray-say-see]

As you know, a *medrese* is a theological school, and although this *medrese* still has the classical atmosphere of 1708 when it was built, it is now a popular café for *nargile* (water pipe) smokers.

Ali Paşa was Sultan Mustafa II's son-in-law and Sultan Ahmet III's Grand Vizier. Originally from Çorlu, a small town on the way to Edirne, he was the son of a barber. (Since there were many Ali Paşas, the word *Çorlulu* indicates that this is the one from Çorlu.) A bright young man, Ali Paşa was brought to study in the Royal Court Academy. In spite of his impressive connections, he was exiled to an island on the Aegean Sea after significant disagreement over his role in a conflict between Sweden and Russia. He was eventually beheaded, in 1711, and his head was returned to Istanbul — reputedly preserved in honey — and buried in the graveyard outside this *medrese,* which he'd had built three years earlier.

The cells of the *medrese,* once peopled with young scholars, are now used as shops for lanterns, rugs and *kilims.* The major focus of this medrese, though, is its *nargile* café.

Tobacco (usually apple-fla-

Entrance to Ali Paşa Medresesi (above); *Nargile* smoker relaxes in the courtyard café (left).

cious stones (which you can admire in the Topkapı Museum). The sweet, heavy scent of apple tobacco infuses the air of this open-air *nargile* café. Perhaps this heady atmosphere will waft you back three centuries to Ali Paşa's time as you soak in the ambience of bright lanterns, intricate *kilims*, and beautifully crafted water pipes.

As you leave the *medrese,* notice the huge tree that has grown inside the first tomb on the left of the exit. As you pass, also note how charcoal is prepared for the *nargiles.*

vored) is rolled into a short, fat cigar and placed in a ceramic container at the top of the water pipe. The tobacco is covered with foil and burning charcoal is set on top of it. As the smoker inhales, the smoke circulates through the water-filled bottle, cooling it before it reaches the smoker's mouth (through a disposable mouthpiece). Sultans used mouthpieces made of amber, often decorated with diamonds or other pre-

 As you leave the *medrese,* turn left toward the tomb across the side street.

KOCA SİNAN PAŞA TÜRBESİ–18A
[koh-JAH see-NAHN pah-SHAH tewr-bay-SEE]

This picturesque *türbe*, or mausoleum, holds the remains of Koca Sinan Paşa, who was a Grand Vizier under Sultan Murat III and Mehmet III. He was also the conqueror of Yemen. The complex, which also includes a *sebil* and *medrese*, was built in 1593. Koca Sinan died two years later. The *türbe* is probably the most impressive part of the complex, with its 16 sides, multicolored marble, ornate windows, and stalactite cornices. The *sebil* has lovely ornate grillwork, through which free drinks were distributed to passersby. It now serves as a refreshment stand, somewhat in keeping with its history.

Retrace your steps along Ordu Caddesi, now called Yeniçeriler Caddesi, and take the first right onto Çarşıkapı Caddesi. Follow that straight ahead, looking for the Sepetçi Han on your left.

SEPETÇİ HAN–19A
[say-payt-CHEE hahn]

This han, which is now mainly a leather bazaar, was most likely established for the makers of baskets (*sepet*). The Sepetçi Han is interesting because the façade of the building still looks very old, while the inside is relatively modern. It was redone in the early 1900s in the Art Deco style by a Frenchman who replaced the heavy colonnades of

yesteryear with thin metal posts and railings. Note that although a roof now covers the courtyard, it still allows natural light to brighten the entire han. The relaxed atmosphere of the courtyard invites merchants and tourists alike to enjoy a glass of tea.

Step back out of the han and take a left. This will take you into the Grand Bazaar. Turn left inside the gate onto Kalpakçılar Caddesi and, just before you get to the next gate (Beyazıt Kapısı), you will see a tiny passageway on your left.

If you'd like to see a spectacular view over the rooftops of the Grand Bazaar, turn into this passage and step into the Nasip Carpet Shop. Though little is known of this building except that it was a workshop for shoemakers, it is beautifully restored and the view is well worth the side trip. If you show them this book, they'll gladly guide you up the three flights of stairs to see the view from their upstairs office. If you're not up for the climb, just continue on to Beyazıt Kapısı (the gate).

Come back out into the bazaar, turn left, and continue on through Beyazıt Kapısı; then turn right on Çadırcılar Caddesi. Continue up that street until you see an awning on your right that says SARNIÇLI HAN with arched windows above it. You can enter this han directly from the street under the awning. The entrance is about six meters before the end of the building.

SARNIÇLI HAN–20A
[sahr-nuhch-LUH hahn]

The Sarnıçlı Han's exterior is true to its original design, although like many hans its interior has been renovated. The open courtyard still has two levels with arched colonnades, though they've been plastered and painted. The han takes its name from a huge cistern (*sarnıç*) in the courtyard. It has been converted to a tea shop, around which you can relax and sip a cup. The floor of the courtyard is all marble. The han also has an ancient underground cistern, which has been covered over because too many people were using it to dump trash. Today the shops in this han sell clothing, rugs and copperware.

As you exit the Sarnıçlı Han, turn right and walk a few blocks further along the street, now Fuat Paşa Caddesi, to Mercan Caddesi. Your final destination on this walk is a small mosque just ahead of you on the intersection of these two streets.

FUAT ALİ PAŞA CAMİSİ (MOSQUE)–21A
[foo-AHT ah-LEE pah-SHAH JAH-mee-see]

This stunning little mosque was built by Fuat Ali Paşa, a Grand Vizier of the 19th century. It boasts a lovely *sebil* and unique decorations like the ornate carving along its cornices and the six-pointed Star of David in the upper windows on each side. This common Jewish symbol is also known as Solomon's (Süleyman's) Seal by Muslims, who see Solomon (the son of David) as a prophet. This dual symbolism demonstrates just how tolerant the

Fuat Ali Paşa Sebili.

Detail of Fuat Ali Paşa minaret balcony (left) and six-pointed star window (below).

Ottoman sultans were of other religions. The mosque has an unusual hexagonal minaret with ornate metal grillwork on the windows to light the staircase leading to the balcony, where the *müezzin* calls the faithful to prayer five times a day.

If you look west across Fuat Paşa Caddesi, you will have another view of Beyazıt Tower through Örücüler Gate to the University.

Congratulations! You've finished the first walk. You will probably be ready to stop for tea or a meal, and you may want to explore the Grand Bazaar. If you still have plenty of energy, take a break and then continue with the second walk, which includes hans in and around the Grand Bazaar.

KEMAL OCAK
Han renovator, Leather merchant, & Restauranteur / Taş Han

Though the Taş Han was a crumbling ruin when Kemal Ocak purchased it, he was able to envision the incredible possibilities of this ancient building that once belonged to the Laleli Mosque complex.

Originally from Artvin, a city near Trabzon, Kemal Bey grew up with four brothers and one sister, working in the family's leather factory. After finishing technical school in Istanbul, Kemal Bey moved to Prague for a short while, then on to Poland. There he met his wife Anna, a teacher. He brought his new wife back to Istanbul, seeking a spot for his leather business. When he saw that the Taş Han was for sale, his imagination soared. This would be his future; he knew the han had great possibilities and he would find a way to restore it.

So the saga began. Kemal Bey convinced his family to purchase the han with him, and in 1987—now with a wife and daughter to support—he dove into the project. After six years of bureaucracy

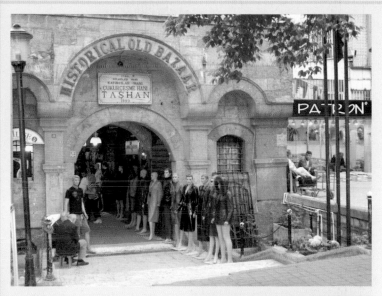

Entrance to renovated Taş Han
(above) and carpet portrait of
Kemal Ocak (below)

and paperwork, Kemal Bey
abandoned his hopes for government funding; all he had
received was their stamp of
approval for the project. Kemal
Bey and his family financed the
entire operation, which often
involved 30 to 40 people working day and night. The restoration was finally completed in
1996 after three years of hard
work.

Kemal Bey became an active
participant in the Laleli community, reaching out to help others as
well as supporting his own project. A handmade carpet portrait of
Kemal Ocak hangs at the top of a spiral staircase in the Taş Han
Restaurant, a gesture of thanks from a family Kemal Ocak aided in
their time of need.

Kemal Bey is the owner/manager of the facility, overseeing the
two restaurants as well as his leather shop. If you can find him
(probably in the Taşhan Restaurant), be sure to greet him and
thank him for his efforts to preserve this bit of Istanbul's past.

RECAİ AND MUSTAFA AKYOL
Booksellers / Sahaflar Han

The Sahaflar Çarşısı is actually more a bazaar than a han. Recai and Mustafa Akyol own Tuğra Antik, a shop on an inside corner of the bazaar at number 41. They sell coins, stamps, old postcards, medals, rosaries, calligraphy, engravings, miniatures, and framed pages from handwritten Ottoman books as well as other sundry items. Their merchandise appeals mainly to tourists and Turkish collectors, while most of the other shops in the bazaar are frequented by Turks.

These brothers have run their shop together for 15 years, both buying and selling souvenirs and collectors' items. They travel nearly an hour from different directions to get to work each day and they are open seven days a week, twelve hours a day (from 8 A.M. to 8 P.M.), like most of the other merchants in this busy market.

ADEM CANTÜRK USTA
Börekçi / Sahaflar Han area

Börek is a deliciously light pastry often made with cheese, potatoes, and sometimes fruit. Simit and börek are staples in Turkey, and Adem Usta is among the best of the *börekçi* (maker and seller of börek).

Although he was born in Istanbul, Adem Bey's family is originally from Erzincan, a city in eastern Turkey. He learned to bake *börek* when he worked for Levon Bey in a tiny restaurant in the Büyük Safran Han (in the Grand Bazaar). For twenty years he served customers and helped in the kitchen. In 1995 when high rents forced Levon to close the restaurant, Adem Usta started making *börek* on his own.

Working out of a small kitchen nearby, Adem Bey gets up at 6 A.M. six days a week to bake his pastries, then carries them out to sell on the street. A big roll of newsprint "napkins" is stuffed into the pocket of his apron as he carries a huge platter piled with pastries on his head. He sets it on a small stool and waits patiently for his wares to disappear, which they do in a heartbeat. Everyone in the area knows Adem Bey and waits for his daily selection of delicious börek. He has long rolls called *sigara böreği*, filled with cheese or potatoes, delicious apple-filled pastries called *elmalı börek*, and other small cakes.

You may be lucky enough to catch Adem Usta on the street, in one of the courtyards, or in the Sahaflar book bazaar. If you do see him, you'll surely want to try his wares.

Nur-u Osmaniye Mosque.

Walk B
In and around the Grand Bazaar

TO BEGIN WALK B:

Take the city tram to the Beyazıt stop, two stops west of Sultanahmet. Go to your left as you exit the tram (west— away from Sultanahmet, toward the large mosque on your left). Cross over the taxi and bus area and walk straight in from the corner. You'll see an expanse of sidewalk and a large entrance to the Grand Bazaar (Beyazıt Kapısı) on your right. Walk past that gate (and past a few smaller gates) up along Çadırcılar Caddesi past many street vendors until you come to Mercan Caddesi. You'll see a university gate on your left and a lovely little two-story mosque on the right.

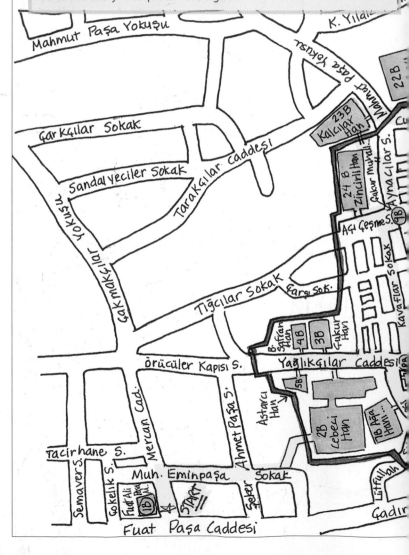

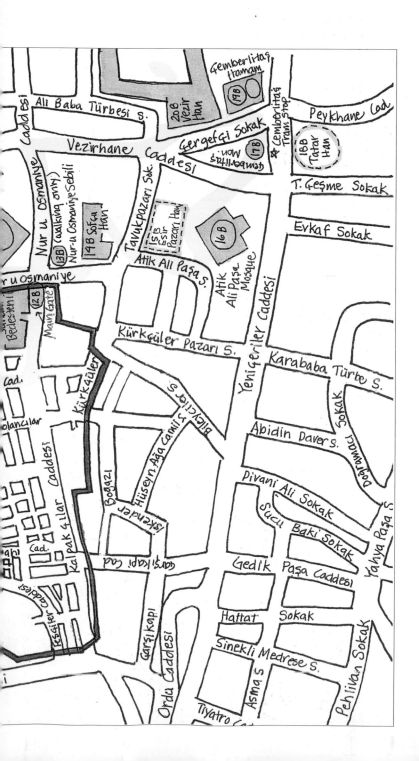

FUAT ALİ PAŞA CAMİSİ (MOSQUE)–1B

For a description of this site, see page 56 at the end of Walk A.

🚶 Turn right along Mercan Caddesi for one block, then turn right and walk one and a half blocks down Mühürdar Eminpaşa Sokak. Watch carefully on your left for a small sign that says CEBECİ HAN over a doorway just before the road takes a turn to the right. Walk through the narrow passage and down a few separate sets of stairs to get to the main courtyard of the han.

CEBECİ HAN–2B
[jeh-beh-JIH hahn]

For general information on hans, see the introduction and the text box on page 26.

After you walk through a narrow passageway, this tiny entrance opens into an ancient han. You will be able to peek into workshops and galleries as you meander down the stairs to the main courtyard of this complicated building. Welcome to the Cebeci Han, a han of the 18th cen-

tury. A shop on the upper balcony displays incredible oversized copper urns, teapots, and ewers. There was once a small pond and a mosque in the courtyard, but the mosque was destroyed in the earthquake of 1894. You must use your imagination to envision it at that time with its arched gallery

surrounding an idyllic courtyard.

This han was once known for its *ramatevi,* where filings of gold and silver from workshops in nearby hans were melted into bars to be reused. Gold and silver workers have wooden or metal grilles on the floor to catch the silver and gold dust that falls to the floor and to protect it from sticking to shoes and being carried away into the street. (You will see these later in workshops along this walk.) When the grille is lifted and the floor is swept, the dust and dirt that has collected is placed into sacks and brought to the *ramatevi,* where the dust is burned away at a very high temperature to reclaim the gold or silver. Unfortunately, that shop has moved; the space is now a carpet shop.

On the ground floor at the end of the courtyard you will see an antique shop displaying metalwares of every kind. You may find some bargains if you take the time to rummage through the heap of antiques. Though the shop owner,

Nizam Çolak, doesn't speak English, he will be happy to show you some of his more interesting items. Next door is his polishing workshop, where he shines brass and copper items for shops in the Grand Bazaar. Here you can have your fine metals polished more cheaply than through a shop. (You'll just eliminate the middleman— your copper would probably have been polished here anyway.) In the 1960s various types of furniture were sold in the shops around the courtyard, but that, too, has changed.

➡ " See profile of leather presser Kenan Kahya on page 96-97."

➡ " See profile of copper worker Nizam Çolak 97."

WC ALERT: The restrooms in the middle of this courtyard are kept very clean and they are easily accessible from the Grand Bazaar. You pay a small fee at the white kiosk near the restrooms.

The far exit from the main courtyard is to the right of the Tuğra Antique Shop. Follow that passageway past a few restaurants; then you will magically find yourself inside the Grand Bazaar. Turn to your left on the first avenue, Yağlıkçılar Sokağı, and you will see the Çukur Han immediately on your right. Look for a simple orange sign above a small arched entrance, as well as a white *Sağlık Ocağı* (health clinic) sign.

ÇUKUR HAN–3B
[choo-KOOR hahn]

The Çukur Han, a quiet haven in the bustling Grand Bazaar, is a relaxed place to look for textiles, *kilims*, and ceramics. Not long ago, cotton was dyed here in the traditional technique. First, yarn was stomped with bare feet (like grapes) in a tub of water until it was thoroughly wet; then it was stirred into boiling dye, rinsed in clear water in a second tub, and spun dry. Lastly, it was hung in a warm room to dry overnight.

Today you will find a variety of textiles displayed in the Çukur Han, as well as some of the finest Kütahya ceramic pieces, each one chosen with care. As you wander through the halls and courtyards of this han, note the pointed-arch colonnades typical of hans from the Ottoman era.

If you climb the stairs at the end of the first corridor, you will discover a lovely grape arbor sitting area near the clinic. You may want to take a moment to rest your feet in this peaceful environment. If Adem Usta should appear with his tray of *börek* (Turkish cheese pastry), be sure to stop him for one. Mention Edda, and he'll surely charm you with his winning smile.

Exit the Çukur Han through the arch you entered, then turn right and follow the same avenue (Yağlıkçılar Sokağı). A few shops up the street you will see another tiny entrance to the Büyük Safran Han on your right about halfway to the exit. Again, look for a rough orange sign high up on the wall.

BÜYÜK SAFRAN HAN–4B
[bew-YEWK sahf-RAHN]

Ottoman cistern in Büyük Safran Han (below); *tavla* players in courtyard (left).

Although this tiny han is hidden away in a corner of the Bazaar and used primarily for storage, you may want to check out its lovely Ottoman fountain, which has been placed against a wall to preserve it. Note the graceful carving in the marble and the iron pump handle hanging beside it. A group of merchants in the bazaar has taken on the project of restoring this fountain to its original beauty (at their own expense). You will most likely come across men playing backgammon, a favorite pastime in this secluded haven. The corner on your left as you enter was once a small restaurant where baker and street merchant Adem Usta learned to bake *börek*.

Slightly to the right across from the Büyük Safran Han you will find the entrance to the Astarcı Han. Walk up the corridor to its large, open courtyard.

ASTARCI HAN–5B
[ahs-tahr-JUH hahn]

In the courtyard of the Astarcı Han, a pump is still used to pull water from an ancient marble cistern into a low marble basin. The workshop in the corner behind it is fascinating. Step inside and note the dozens of glittering spools that line the wall. If the machines are in action, you will see how gold trimmings are made

Gold braids emerge from spinning spools (above); Ottoman fountain and cistern in Astarcı Han courtyard (left)

from these wildly spinning spools. You can buy them for clothing or Christmas parcels at half the price you would pay in a shop.

Although most of the original grillwork in the archways of this han has been plastered over, you will see occasional signs of its fine craftsmanship.

As you exit the Astarcı Han turn right onto Yağlıkçılar Sokağı and follow it beyond the entrance into the Cebeci Han (now on your right). Take the next right onto Yorgancılar Caddesi. About five meters on your left is a small entryway into the Evliya Han, marked only with a WC sign. Walk through this entrance (as though you know what you're doing) and into the open courtyard, where you'll find one of the bazaar's small mosques.

EVLİYA HAN–6B
[ev-lee-AH hahn]

This tucked-away han has its original Ottoman fountain, where you will see bazaar merchants, craftsmen, and shoppers making their ablutions before prayer. They will then climb the staircase around the corner to a simple mosque located on the second floor of this lovely hideaway. Recent renovations have been true to the original design, with arched colonnades typical of most Ottoman hans. Though the mosque is small and plain, it serves the needs of local merchants well.

Step back outside the Evliya Han and take a left again on Yorgancılar Caddesi, then take the first right turn through an archway into the Ağa Han (Hatip Emin Han).

AĞA HAN (HATİP EMİN HAN)–7B
[ah-AH hahn / hah-TEEP ay-MEEN hahn]

The Turkish word *ağa* is an honorary title referring to the "chief" or "master" of the sultan's eunuchs or of a military squadron, the person who most likely built this han. It is organized around a huge Ottoman fountain, always a focal point for ancient hans, which as you recall were used as inns. Note the Ottoman script carved into the side of the marble basin beside the cistern.

Ottoman fountain (above) and detail of Ottoman script from its marble basin (below)

Retrace your steps back to Yağlıkçılar Sokağı and take a right. Follow this street until you meet a main crossing, at Kavaflar Sokağı. Mounted high on the right wall you'll see a green pulpit-like structure used as a minaret. To the right of it a stairway leads to a small upstairs mosque.

CAFER AĞA CAMİSİ (MOSQUE)–8B
[jah-FAYR ah-AH JAH-mee-see]

Cafer Ağa Mosque is one of a few small mosques within the walls of the bazaar, but it definitely has the prettiest *şerefe* (balcony surrounding a minaret), from where the *müezzin* recites the call to prayer. This is a landmark on the west side of the bazaar. If you visit the bazaar again, it may help you get your bearings to find your way through the streets that make up the ever confusing maze of the Grand Bazaar.

Cafer Ağa Mosque looks straight down Kavaflar Sokağı. Walk down that street three blocks until you reach a T-Intersection. Look to your right and you'll see a dark brown freestanding kiosk with an onion dome, built in the middle of the passage. Turn toward it.

ÇUKUR MUHALLEBİCİSİ–9B
[choo-KOOR moo-HAHL-lay-bee-jee-SEE]

Front and rear views of Çukur Muhallebicisi.

This charming kiosk, built around 1850, was once a famous pastry shop, though it has since been converted to a jewelry and souvenir shop. According to legend, the sultan sometimes shared tea with his friends in a second-story room, watching over the activity in the bazaar. The word "Salon" beside the ornate upper entrance at the top of the stairs indicates where they may have sat. Whether this tale is true or not, it's intriguing to imagine a sultan who enjoyed this "bird's-eye view" of his subjects at their daily tasks.

Continue past the kiosk up along Kuyumcular Caddesi until you see an entrance on your right leading into the oldest section of the Grand Bazaar.

CEVAHİR BEDESTENİ
(OLD BAZAAR, ANTIQUE BAZAAR)–10B
[jay-vah-HEER bay-day-stay-NEE]

A bas-relief eagle, a relic from the Byzantine Empire, guards this Gate of the Goldsmiths entrance to the Cevahir Bedesteni. *Cevahir* means gems or precious stones and a *bedesten* is a fire-proof, vaulted section of a bazaar where valuable goods are kept. (Though the sign above the entrance is spelled with an "a," the correct spelling is *bedesten*.)

Sultan Mehmet II, also known as Mehmet the Conqueror (Fatih), had this building erected on the site of a similar Byzantine market

building just three years after he conquered Constantinople in 1453. One wonders if he had any idea that it would be famous for centuries after his death. Four years later the sultan had a similar building built a little further away toward the east, the Sandal Bedesteni.

The Cevahir Bedesteni, now mainly an antique market, is considered the oldest section of the Grand Bazaar and is consequently called "The Old Bedesten." Inside the building there is a wooden gallery just under the windows from which the watchman could easily open and close the windows as well as watch over the treasures of this market.

Bedesten

Since the first days of their construction, *bedesten*s housed the most precious wares; they were also used as a treasury for valuables belonging to viziers (ministers) and prominent people, much like a hired safe or bank. Because this area was well guarded, it soon became crowded with

merchants who wanted to take advantage of that security. A row of shops was built against the outer walls, then a second row was built opposite the first one, and soon a third one leaning against the second one, forming haphazard streets with no definite plan.

The shops inside the *bedesten*s looked like cupboards lying sideways. (You can see one in the Islamic Arts Museum.) One door of the cupboard lifted up and had a few shelves to display goods; the other door was part of a chest that held the merchandise, and the merchant stood behind it. Consequently an Ottoman woman did not need to go into a shop, because the cabinet served as an open shop.

Antiques displayed in the Antique Bazaar.

As in today's street markets, a cloth awning was stretched over the streets around the *bedesten*s to protect shoppers and merchandise from the elements. Up through the 18th century, hans were built surrounding these streets, thus forming a boundary to the market streets. Finally brick domes were added overhead, hence the Turkish name for the Grand Bazaar: Kapalı Çarşı (Covered Bazaar).

goods were displayed, which certainly must have allowed greater government control. The streets still bear the names of each guild, like "polishers" or "pearl sellers." Very strict rules were observed; a merchant who had a shop on his designated street could not open business premises on another, nor could he sell wares other than those of his guild. Women were never allowed to be shopkeepers (and even today, few run shops in Turkey).

Guilds

Similar to the Byzantine system of commercial organization, the Ottoman market was organized by guilds. Not just collections of related workers and artisans, the guilds of the Grand Bazaar were tightly knit communities of experts in their fields. They included initiation rites, apprenticeships, cradle-to-grave security, and shared religious habits. Each trade had its own exclusive areas where similar

A rare sculpture of an eagle graces the entrance to the Cevahir Bedesteni.

If you look up in the center of the Old Bedesten, you will see a tiny wooden mosque situated above the shops—yet another example of the importance of religion to Ottoman Muslims. Note the lovely stained-glass tulip windows and miniature minaret. Note, too, the beautiful circular brickwork of the domes of the *bedesten*'s ceiling, a work of art in itself.

Find your way back to the Eagle Entrance (straight down from the miniature mosque) and turn right onto Kuyumcular Caddesi, which changes its name to Terzi Başı Aralığı. Follow it three blocks until you reach the main street on the south side of the bazaar, Kalpakçılar Caddesi, or Gold Street. This is a wide, very straight street, and you can see the exit down the street on your left. Turn left onto this street and take the second left turn, which will lead you down a stairway into the second bedesten of the Grand Bazaar.

SANDAL BEDESTENİ–11B
[sahn-DAHL bay-day-stay-NEE]

This great hall, with its 12 massive piers supporting 20 domes, is called Sandal Bedesteni after a very heavy and precious cloth that was woven in Bursa, the center of Turkey's yarn and textile trade for centuries. This *bedesten* was the market for precious textiles. Under light filtering through its tall, arched windows, dozens of varieties of fabric were displayed, some embroidered with real jewels. Many hung full-length from the heavy piers, while others were spread across counters, twinkling and reflecting light in every shade imaginable. To the eyes of visiting foreigners, these fabrics glowed like the stained-glass windows of cathedrals. It continues to sell mainly textiles, though there is certainly a more modern variety available—along with many souvenirs.

This *bedesten* was cleaned after a fire, so it looks quite new.

Midweek auctions were held here from 1914 through the 1980s, an exciting event at the Grand Bazaar. The afternoon auctions offered different items each day. Anyone could bring items to be sold, and they were evaluated and displayed in windows the day before the auction, for which a small fee was charged. You could come to watch an auction just for the fun of it but, as with most auctions, unsuspecting observers sometimes made unintentional bids by merely scratching a nose, ear, or head.

Once you've finished exploring this fascinating section of the bazaar, exit the way you entered, onto the main street of the Grand Bazaar, Kalpakçılar Caddesi. Take a left and it will lead you out the bazaar's main gate.

GRAND BAZAAR (KAPALI ÇARŞI—COVERED BAZAAR) MAIN GATE–12B
[kah-pah-LUH chahr-SHUH]

The main gate to the Grand Bazaar (Kapalı Çarşı or Covered Bazaar) is decorated with a coat of arms containing flags, books, a horn of plenty, a scale, and arms (symbolic of the Ottoman sultan's power). It was built in the 19th century and shows strong European influence, although the design is reminiscent of a turban crest made of enamel, pearls, rubies and emeralds. (The sultan didn't wear a crown but a turban with a crest made of gems.)

First built over 450 years ago, the bazaar has 15 other gates (plus those of hans leading into the bazaar) and consists of over 4000 shops. It covers 37,000 square meters, or about nine acres. Its appearance is very similar to what it was centuries ago, in spite of the fact that parts of it have been destroyed by fire. The interior is loosely organized, with certain types of merchandise sold in separate areas of the bazaar. For instance, mostly jewelry is sold on the main street you just walked through, leather is sold mostly on the south side of the main street, rugs are in the central area, etc. Incidentally, more than half of the shops are devoted to the weighing, shaping, and selling of gold. A fascinating labyrinth of 60-odd streets, Istanbul's Kapalı Çarşı is one of the best-known bazaars in the world.

Just outside the main gate to the right across the street is a lovely grilled *sebil* hung with carpets and *kilims*.

NUR-U OSMANİYE SEBİLİ–13B
[noor-OO ohs-mah-nee-yay say-bee-LEE]

For more information on sebils, see the text box on page 31.

dation by the Belli family, who rent it from the government for their carpet business (Anatolian Carpets, *Kilims* & Sumaks). They had the *sebil* restored at their own expense in the late 1990s, paying meticulous attention to original detail from a 1900 photo (below).

This famous *sebil* is a part of the Nur-u Osmaniye *külliye* (mosque complex). Inside the *sebil* is a lovely Ottoman fountain that provided the water shared with the public at the expense of Sultan Mahmut I and his brother and successor, Osman III (mid-1700s). The name Nur-u Osmaniye means "sacred light of Osman," referring to Osman, the founder of the Ottoman Empire. This *sebil* was saved from dilapi-

➡ " See profile of carpet dealer Celal Belli on page 98."

➡ " See profile of carpet dealer Celal Belli on page 98."

Continue up the street on your right, along the side of the Bazaar, about a half block to a very old archway on your left. Two marble steps will lead you into what's left of the Sofçu Han.

SOFÇU HAN–14B
[sohf-CHOO hahn]

We are going through what used to be the Sofçu Han of the 18th century and we can only guess at its past beauty from what remains. Look up and you'll note that the ancient archways offer an interesting contrast to the Nur-u Osmaniye Mosque behind it. It must have been a han for the manufacture or sale of *sof*, woolen cloth or raw silk.

Step down through the courtyard, which has been redone with a marble fragment floor. Savor the delectable smells of this han, which is now filled with small restaurants rather than the wool and silk shops its name comes from.

> Walk up the stairs on the far end of the courtyard. Notice the many domes and chimneys of the Nur-u Osmaniye Medresesi on your left. This was once a theological school for young men.

> As you exit the Sofçu Han, you'll see a large parking lot ahead of you to the left. Straight ahead of you on the right (west of the parking lot) is a series of small shops. This is where the Esir Pazarı Hanı once stood.

ESİR PAZARI HANI–15B
[ay-SEER pah-zah-RUH hahn]

At one time, the Esir Pazarı Hanı was situated beyond the Sofçu Han. Built in the 15th century, it was a center for the buying and selling of slaves, usually brought back from Ottoman conquests. The best of the slaves were kept for the sultan, while the others were sold to the highest bidder. The han was reputed to have 300 rooms in its two stories and, like many hans, it had a gate with iron locks. The han was guarded by an inspector who demanded a tithe from each slave sale. This commerce was forbidden in the 19th century by Sultan Abdülmecit (who had the Dolmabahçe Palace built). Although we all applaud the end of slavery, it's unfortunate that no trace of the han remains.

> Walk straight ahead between the shops and the parking lot, and at the end of the walkway you will see a stairway to a large mosque.

ATİK ALİ PAŞA CAMİSİ (MOSQUE)–16B
[ah-TEEK ah-lee pah-SHAH JAH-mee-see]

This mosque, also called "Sedefçiler [mother-of-pearl craftsmen] Mosque," was built in 1496, making it one of the oldest mosques in the city. It was built by Hadım (eunuch) Atik Ali Paşa, who was Grand Vizier to Sultan Beyazıt II, the son of Sultan Mehmet the Conqueror. It is surrounded by a lovely, quiet garden that separates it from the busy street. Its *külliye* (mosque complex) once included a *tekke* (dervish lodge), an *imaret* (soup kitchen), a han and a *medrese* (a theological school), but these have all been destroyed.

> Cross or walk around the big parking lot to the tall structure on Ordu Caddesi. This monument has been under renovation and behind scaffolding for decades, but perhaps you will be fortunate enough to see it in its full glory.

ÇEMBERLİTAŞ COLUMN (BURNT COLUMN)–17B
[chaym-bayr-lee-tahsh]

This column marks the center of what was once the forum of Constantine the Great, erected by him to celebrate the dedication of the city as capital of the declining Roman Empire on May 11, A.D. 330. He named the city *Nea Roma* (New Rome), but his people loved him so much, they preferred calling it Constantinopolis (Constantine's City). The oval-shaped forum was surrounded by columned porticoes. This central column consists of six porphyry (red marble) drums. Some joints between them were hooped in the fifth century with iron bands, which were replaced in the 18th century. This is why it is called Çemberlitaş, which means

the guise of a radiant Apollo with the face of Constantine. Made of gold, it fell in 1106 during a storm, crushing several passersby to death. Some 50 years later, Emperor Manuel Comnenus replaced it with a large gold cross, which was removed during the Ottoman period.

Constantine not only tolerated Christianity but also encouraged it; even before he was a Christian himself, he is thought to have declared it the state religion. (Some sources say that Theodosius I made Christianity the state religion.) Wanting to please both the pagan senate and the numerous Christians as well, he had a small edifice erected near the foot of the column, in which was kept a collection of relics of the three religions: paganism, Christianity, and Judaism. Reputedly, these included the Palladium (Pallas's wooden statue, which had assured Troy's safety), Noah's hatchet, the stone from which Moses made water flow, the remains of the loaves with which Christ fed the multitude (with one of the original baskets), a gown of the Virgin, pieces of the True Cross, a nail from the cross, and the Crown of Thorns. Constantine did not declare himself a Christian until he was 40 years old and, like many Christians of that time, he wasn't baptized until just before his death, in 337.

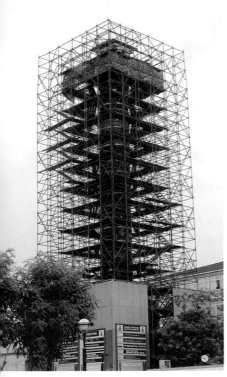

Çemberlitaş Column under renovation.

"hooped column." They also call it the "burnt column," because of the many great fires which destroyed much of the surrounding area, blackening the monument's marble surface.

On the large marble capital stood a statue of Constantine, in

Looking across the main street a century ago, you would have seen a beautiful old han that served an important role during Ottoman times. Unfortunately, it has been displaced by more modern buildings, now the *Kültür Merkezi*.

After you leave this area, look back at the monument from a distance and you will be able to glimpse it through the scaffolding.

ELÇİ HAN—TATAR HAN–18B
[ayl-CHEE hahn]

The pink building across the main street from the Çemberlitaş Column was built on the site of the old Elçi Han. *Elçi* means ambassador and ambassadors stayed here until the end of the 17th century, when most of the new embassies were built in Pera on the other side of the Golden Horn. Because of the importance of the personages residing in the han, one needed written permission to go into or out of the building. It had two kitchens and stables for 400 horses, although it had no storage rooms since the ambassadors brought no merchandise. Planks were nailed over the windows to keep these foreign dignitaries from peering into the latticed windows of the second-story harems of neighboring houses.

This han was built by Hadım (eunuch) Atik Ali Paşa in 1510 and was part of the complex of his nearby mosque (which you just saw). Once the ambassadors moved to the other side of the Golden Horn at the beginning of the 19th century, Tatar (Tartar) postmen began lodging in the Elçi Han. Consequently, it was renamed the Tatar Han.

Across the side street to the east of the column, look up to see that the entire corner is a two-domed structure. The unassuming entrance to this ornate *hamam* faces you just a few shops to the left of the corner.

ÇEMBERLİTAŞ HAMAMI (OF NUR BANU HATUN)–19B
[chaym-bayr-lee-tahsh hah-mahm-UH]

The mothers of sultans were powerful women. (The word "sultan" appeared at the end of their name rather than before it, as in the case of their sons.) The *hamam* of Nur Banu Hatun Valide Sultan, the mother of Sultan Murat III, was built in 1584 by the great architect Sinan, who built the famous Süleymaniye Mosque. He also built a second *hamam* for her on the Golden Horn.

The double domes indicate that there were separate sections for men and women, with entrances on different façades. The women's entrance has been transformed into a restaurant, so both men and women now use the original men's entrance, which faces the Çemberlitaş Column. Much of the marble work on the interior of the baths is still original, complete with ornate carving on each of the separate washing cells. It's fascinating to visit a

Çemberlitaş Hamam (above) and its inside entrance (right).

hamam to refresh and relax after a long day of exploring in Istanbul. (Where else can you rest on a heated marble slab?)

According to tradition, Ottoman men and women went separately to the *hamam* to be washed before a feast or a wedding. Since only the wealthiest homes were equipped with private baths, the vast majority of citizens used the *hamam*, not only to clean themselves but also as a distraction. For most women, it was their only outing without a male chaperone. Often the mother of a young man would watch a

prospective daughter-in-law's behavior in the local *hamam* to make sure that she was fit for her son and would suit her as a daughter before taking steps to have the marriage arranged.

Standing across the street from the *hamam* entrance, look to your left at the top of the ancient building next to the *hamam*. This is the Vezir Han. Follow the street toward it for a half block and on your right you will see an ancient arch over a path into the han courtyard.

VEZİR HAN–20B
[vay-ZEER hahn]

The Vezir Han was built near the Elçi Han by the eminent Köprülü family, from whose ranks came most of the Grand Viziers between 1656 and 1735. It was built specifically for use by provincial governors and their servants. The han's monumental gate is intricately decorated with floral tile work and a green crest with Ottoman script in gold and the ceiling of the entrance has been repainted with ornate floral designs. As you enter, note the huge doors that could be closed and locked at night to protect the residents of the han. A few paces forward on your right, there is a Corinthian capital (recycled from the Forum of Constantine) now

used as a base for the wall next to a barbershop. If you look to your right after you pass the barbershop, a stairway leads to an area that looks much like it must have in the 17th century when this han was bustling with activity.

Straight ahead you'll enter the courtyard, one of the largest in

Corinthian column incorporated into wall (above) and inner courtyard of the Vezir Han (below).

Detail of ceiling in entrance to han (above) and stairway leading to upper story of han (right).

Istanbul. You can see why the darker and windowless lower levels were used as stables and storerooms, while the second level, more open and light, was used for living quarters. There was once a small mosque in the center of the courtyard, similar to most large hans of the time. Since they were seldom repaired, few of these mosques have survived.

Exit the Vezir Han and take a right again on this street, Vezirhan Caddesi. Walk up to the second left turn, an archway leading into the courtyard of a huge mosque. (A wide mall of exclusive shops leads up to your right across from the archway.) Walk through the courtyard as you admire this impressive structure.

NUR-U OSMANİYE CAMİSİ (MOSQUE)–21B
[noor-OO ohs-mah-nee-yay JAH-mee-see]

As with the *sebil*, this mosque was built in honor of Osman, who founded the Ottoman Empire. The building of this mosque was initiated by Sultan Mahmut I in 1748 and finished by his brother and successor Sultan Osman III in 1755. It is a baroque mosque of the same period as the Laleli Mosque, and it's probably the busiest mosque in the city because of its location directly outside the Grand Bazaar's main gate, Nur-u Osmaniye Kapısı. The walkway alongside the mosque is always teeming with people selling their wares, waiting for friends, or just resting their weary feet on the very welcome benches provided there.

Follow the walkway to the main gate of the Bazaar (and bid it yet another hello). But before entering the bazaar, turn right along the cobbled street lined with shops, Nur-u Osmaniye Sokak. When the road turns to the right, step instead into the bazaar through the gate on your left, the Kilitçiler Kapısı. This banking area is known as the "Open-Air Istanbul Stock Exchange," where many men on cell phones are buying and selling foreign currency and gold. Stay to your right and walk one block, taking the next right out through an arched entrance into the Çuhacı Han. Notice the huge marble archway and worn marble threshold. Prepare to be amazed at the quality of the merchandise and craftsmanship displayed in this han.

ÇUHACI HAN (GOLD HAN)–22B
[choo-hah-JUH hahn]

The Çuhacı Han was built in the 18th century by Sultan Ahmet III's son-in-law, Damat İbrahim Paşa. *Çuha* is a type of broadcloth and this han was originally the cloth merchants' han, although it is now the home of gold smelters as well as many jewelry workshops. It contains more than 300 ateliers (artisans' workshops) as well as six gold-melting forges and scores of wholesale shops. The many beribboned gold coins you see on display are a favorite gift for weddings, anniversaries, births, and circumcision ceremonies. These coins hold their value and can be easily converted to currency, which makes them a simple, popular gift.

There was a small mosque in the courtyard, and when it was damaged after an earthquake, merchants immediately constructed small shops with tarred dome roofs, cluttering the courtyard. Instead of the open feeling of many hans, this one feels a bit claustrophobic with its many gold outlets, until you mount the stairs to the second level. Once there, you can enjoy the view of this unique han, dominated from the south by the Nur-u Osmaniye Mosque, well worth a photo or two.

If you follow the small passageways at the corners of the second level, you will discover some of the gold forges and perhaps a few jewelry workshops where craftsmen are industriously embedding precious jewels into

their settings. Some of these workshops are located on the floor above the second-story gallery as well. Artisans feel privileged to be able to work so close to the Grand Bazaar, where there is always work for them. When they started renting these rooms as workshops,

Jewelry worker and gold displays in gold han.

keeps feeding the gold into smaller and smaller grooves until it reaches the size required for a particular jewelry project. If the cylinders have no grooves, the result is a long, thin ribbon of gold.

➡ " See profile of stone setter Kaya Değirmenci on page 99."

➡ " See profile of gold and silver smelters Avidis Ağdamar and Erdal Gürkaya on page 100."

telephones were not yet in use, so the closer they were to the Bazaar, the more likely they were to get orders. If you are lucky, you will be able to watch the jewelers at work. Pick up a business card so you can get your jewelry repaired at much less than the cost charged by jewelry shops.

Another interesting activity you may see is the process of melting gold into small bars, then re-forming it into gold wire or ribbon. The cooled gold bar is fed between two rolling drums with different-sized grooves. As it passes between the drums, the gold is pressed into a narrower, thinner, and longer length of gold. The craftsman

Exit the Çuhacı Han and turn right just outside the gate. Follow Çuhacı Han Sokak and walk a block until it comes to a T, with Mahmut Paşa Kapısı on your right. Turn right through that gate, then take an immediate left into a passage behind the gate, which will lead you straight into the Kalcılar Han.

KALCILAR HAN–23B
[kahl-juh-LAHR hahn]

This is the "Silver Han," where the specialty is decorating silver bowls, cups, vases, etc. After the silver is molded into the general desired shape, it is filled with tar before being worked. Once the soft tar cools, designs are made by hitting the objects lightly with different-sized tools. You will find a great variety of silver objects in the shops on the ground floor, while most of the workshops are on the second floor.

In one workshop silver is formed in sand molds. These molds, which are made of two similar pieces, are filled with a very fine mixture of humid sand and soot. It is pressed firmly into one half of the mold; then the article to be reproduced is laid into it. The second half of the mold is placed on top, and the remaining cavity is filled very firmly with more of the sand mixture (to avoid even the tiniest air bubble). When the two halves are opened, the original object is carefully removed and the two halves are reassembled, leaving a hollow space in the form of that object. The forms are stacked one upon the other, making up columns of forms held firmly in place by iron bars. Melted brass, copper, or sil-

Silver worker pounds low-relief scenes into silver (on soft tar).

ver is poured into these molds through the opening, which looks like the neck of a bottle. When the metal has cooled, the molds are opened, the sand poured into a big basin to reuse later, and the various articles removed. These roughly molded articles then move on to the next workshop, either a silversmith or a polisher, who will finish them to send on to a silver or souvenir merchant.

Although most of the trade in this han is wholesale, you may find a bargain as you browse through the shops, where there are often craftsmen at work (as in Barocco on the second floor).

➡ " See profile of silversmith Aruş Taş on page 101."

As you descend the stairs toward the entrance to the Kalcılar Han, watch for a few concrete stairs leading up to your right (just beyond the Tavra Silver Shop). Follow this passage (Sıra Odalar) past Arse Gümüş and take a left where a sign says "Exit" Kapalı Çarşı. You will go down a very narrow passage that leads back into the bazaar. Magic! Turn right and walk along Aynacılar Sokağı to the onion-domed kiosk, where you will take another right. Watch for a large green overhead arrow pointing to the entrance to the Zincirli Han on your right, just before the street turns to the left.

ZİNCİRLİ HAN–24B
[zeen-jeer-LEE hahn]

The pink Zincirli Han, dating back to the end of the 18th century, is one of the most picturesque of Istanbul's many hans. A peaceful haven from the bustle of the bazaar, it has a well-worn stone courtyard with an ornately decorated marble fountain. Quaint gargoyles serve as waterspouts under the eaves, and trees and vines grant welcome shade and attract songbirds to this serene setting. One sometimes sees shopkeepers relaxing together, sipping tea as they watch a friendly game of *tavla* (backgammon).

You may wish to chat with Şişko Osman (Osman-le-Gros), who has an impressive collection of antique rugs in numerous shops on the ground level of this han. After exploring the courtyard, find your way to the stairs just inside the han's entrance.

The steep stairs leading to the second level are worn from centuries of artisans climbing up and down with their wares. Ascend carefully to the second level of this tastefully renovated han to enjoy the serene view over the courtyard and peek into the workshops of the han's jewelers and goldsmiths.

Many of this han's artisans are of Armenian and Jewish descent, and those who speak English will gladly engage in conversation about their trade and their lives. Turkish hospitality, you know. Enjoy!

Ottoman fountain in center of court-yard (above) and Şişko Osman Carpet shop (below).

➡ " See profile of pressed metal artisan Bedros Muratyan on page 132-133."

Whew! You've now finished the second walking tour. It may be time to relax with a glass of tea, or perhaps you'd like to steep in the heat of the Çemberlitaş Hamamı. If you have the energy, you can take a break, then continue on the third walk, which will take you down the hill behind the Grand Bazaar.

KENAN KÂHYA
Leather Dying & Pressing / Cebeci Han

As a boy, Kenan Kâhya worked in a shop where he learned to make metal desks and tables. During his midday break every day he went to help his father dye leather in his Cebeci Han shop, making it clear where his interests lay. Soon he became his father's assistant, dying leather in huge tubs, then ironing it flat for leatherworkers to craft into jackets, coats, rugs, and other clothing.

Kenan Bey still keeps the old wooden leather-pressing machine. It's a huge press with a glass roller that runs back and forth across the leather to flatten it, and he's happy to demonstrate how it works. Although there is little demand for leather-pressing today, he still occasionally dyes leather jackets on order.

Kenan Bey maintains the shop in a corner on the upper floor of the Cebeci Han (number 55), which you can find on the upstairs passageway between the Cebeci and Astarcı Hans. He loves his beautiful spot and has found a way to stay there; he keeps a few chairs and tables on the terrace and serves tea, coffee, fruit, and whatever he has cooked for his own midday meal to other merchants and passersby. Of course, he also offers the ever popular *nargile* (water pipe) as well as a game of *tavla* (backgammon).

Kenan Bey fondly remembers the variety of shops and workshops that filled the Cebeci Han through the '70s: shoemakers, leather sellers, *yorgancı* (men who made quilts filled with cotton wool and sewn with lovely designs), armchair and furniture makers, and many copper workers. As many craftsmen have seen, times are changing, and so is life in the hans. Though his trade hasn't survived these changes, Kenan Kâhya certainly has.

NİZAM ÇOLAK
Copper Worker / Cebeci Han

Nizam Çolak has a business at the far end of the lower courtyard in the Cebeci Han, where he has crafted and polished copper since 1978. After he finished primary school, he learned his trade by working (with his elder brother) as an apprentice to a coppersmith near the Cebeci Han. His antique shop is filled with copper items of all kinds, many of which he has refurbished or repaired—his favorite part of this trade is renewing the life of old and broken copper pieces.

Nizam Bey enjoys the uncluttered light-filled courtyard of the Cebeci Han, where he works six days a week with a part time assistant. Unfortunately, there is not as much demand for the services of a coppersmith today as there once was. Of course, he still loves his work, and his open schedule gives him time to while away the hours with friends playing *tavla* (backgammon), one of the simple joys of life in Istanbul.

CELAL BELLİ
Carpet Dealer / Nur-u Osmaniye Sebil

The man with the brightest smile as you leave the Grand Bazaar's main gate is surely Celal Belli, whose family has sold rugs just outside the Grand Bazaar for generations. His grandfather started the business in 1920 (Anatolian Carpets, *Kilims* & Sumaks), but the most unique thing about their business is that one of their shops is the Nur-u Osmaniye Sebil.

If you step over to the *sebil*, Celal (or whoever is in charge at the moment) will happily show you the fountain inside that for centuries served water to shoppers as they entered or left the Grand Bazaar. Inside the *sebil* there is also an impressive display of historical artifacts, including antique cups that held the precious water.

The family began renting the *sebil* from the state in 1995, but it was in shocking disrepair. "We often sat in the shop with umbrellas when it rained," he said, "and one day, ...shlp ...shlp ...shlp ...both water and ceiling fragments fell on my balding head." He knew that if they didn't do something to restore the building soon, it would collapse on them. They spent a full year restoring the *sebil*: rebuilding the domed roof (with *kilims* under the lead covering on the dome),

repairing the crack in its façade (from an earthquake), and restoring the marble carving around its front grilles. The results are remarkable, as are their many rugs. Although Celal Bey has fond memories of rug-buying excursions across Anatolia in past years, buyers now deliver rugs to them at their shop. The Belli family has two other storefronts, one across the street from the *sebil* and another (a former cistern) next to the Atik Ali Paşa Mosque.

KAYA DEĞİRMENCİ
Stone Setter / Çuhacı Han

Kaya Değirmenci is a master stone setter (jeweler) whose shop on the upper story of the Çuhacı Han employs a range of men eager to learn the trade. Six to eight artisans sit at a long table with electric tools hanging above them and other hand tools arranged across the table, while assistants work at tables elsewhere in the room.

The workshop is like a school for those who want to learn the trade. According to ability and patience, each learns at his own pace and develops his own style. It's not easy to discern the difference between the assistants, apprentices, and masters until you take time to watch them at their trade. In order to most efficiently set stones, jewelry is pressed into a waxen "handle" to make it easier to work the metals and securely fasten gems into their settings.

Kaya Bey has occupied this shop for 30 years, working from 9 a.m. to 7 p.m. six days a week. Sometimes he stays until 11 p.m. to finish his work when it piles up. This is one trade that continues to be in great demand, particularly so close to the Grand Bazaar.

Check it out at #41 Çuhacı Han.

AVİDİS AĞDAMAR & ERDAL GÜRKAYA
Gold & Silver Smelters / Çuhacı Han

Avidis Ağdamar has a shop in an upstairs corner of the Çuhacı Han (number 12). Working with one assistant (his son is still in high school), he melts silver and gold, forming it into bars, which are then pressed and stretched into wires and ribbons for jewelry making. He charges only for his labor, as people bring him the silver or gold that they want formed. There are grilles on the floor to catch fragments of the fine metals. These grilles are lifted weekly and the floor is swept to collect the gold or silver. Once there is enough, it is brought to a smelter who will burn off the dust and melt the metal back into bars for sale.

Erdal Gürkaya, one of the youngest businessmen in the Çuhacı Han, learned this trade after he finished primary school in 1989. He took a position at the Çuhacı Han as a young assistant to a gold smelter, then worked as an apprentice, and finally became the young manager of his workshop. He gets up at 6:00 each morning to come to work (except Sundays) and he runs every phase of the business, from stoking the forge to melting gold in tiny smelting pots; from training his staff to keeping the books. (He finds bookkeeping the most arduous part of his week.) Once the gold is melted, he and his assistants pour it into bar-shaped molds, then reshape it into varying widths of gold wire or gold ribbon for jewelry making.

ARUŞ TAŞ
Silversmith / Kalcılar Han

On an upstairs corner of the Kalcılar Han, Aruş Taş crafts and sells fine silver. In his downstairs shop and upstairs workshop, Barocco, you will find him and his nephews working with silver every day except Sunday. Aruş Bey learned his craft from his *usta* (master), Baruyr Ortainceyan. Hanging on the wall in the upstairs workshop is a unique profile of Mustafa Kemal Atatürk done in silver by Mr. Taş.

Stop by the upstairs Barocco workshop to see these artisans crafting silver. Though Aruş Bey speaks no English, his nephew Arman Taş does, and he will gladly explain the process if you ask. Note the leather aprons (attached to the workbench) worn to catch silver filings, which will be gathered and remelted into bars for new silver pieces. These silversmiths create everything except jewelry, with 50% of the work their own designs. All their items are made with 9.25 carat sterling silver. In addition to a vast array of silver pieces, the shop features a wall of ornate silver mirrors common in Muslim countries because human images were at one time forbidden. The small, typically oval mirrors hang from a chain with the glass against the wall and the ornately worked patterns on their backs facing out.

Sultanahmet Mosque.

Walk C
Behind the Grand Bazaar

TO BEGIN WALK C:

Take the city tram from Eminönü or Sultanahmet to the Çemberlitaş stop. There, get off the tram and follow the street just east of the huge Çemberlitaş Column: Çergeçfi Sokak, the street with shops along the right side and a parking lot on the left. Walk up two blocks until you see a huge mall/sidewalk heading uphill to your right and a stone archway to your left. Turn left here and walk through the Nur-u Osmaniye Mosque courtyard, which will lead you to the main entrance of the Grand Bazaar. Enter the Grand Bazaar (noting the beautiful decorations above the gate) and follow the main road (Kalpakçılar Caddesi) straight. Turn right on the third street, Terzi Başı Aralığı. (It later becomes Kuyumcular and Acı Çeşme Sokağı.) Follow that road straight, passing the dark brown, onion-domed kiosk (see B9) to the north end of the bazaar. Before the street turns to the left, watch for a large green arrow above you pointing to the entrance to the Zincirli Han on your right.

For general information on hans, see the introduction and the text box on page 26.

ZİNCİRLİ HAN–1C
[zeen-jeer-LEE hahn]

For a description of this site (if you didn't do the previous walk), just turn to page 94 at the end of walk B.

 Exit the Zincirli Han and take a right through the Mercan Kapısı. Take your first right into the han just a few shops beyond the gate.

İMAM ALİ HAN–2C
[ee-mahm ah-LEE hahn]

İmam Ali Han was once famous for its archaic handloom, which is unfortunately no longer there. Not too long ago, one could watch a weaver making shawls, deftly stepping on a different pedal each time he pulled yarn through the weft. He synchronized his movements with great care, producing 36 beautiful shawls a day, which were sold in a little shop down the alley.

At the end of the courtyard on the left you can see gold being melted and poured into molds. It is then pressed between cylinders until it becomes a length of wire or long and thin like ribbon. After that it is skillfully crafted by jewelers into rings, chains, and other fine adornments.

Although there is little information about the history of this han, much of the original exterior construction is visible on the upper levels, indicating that it was constructed in the 19th century. On the right side of the courtyard you can still see much of the original stone masonry.

Straight across the street and slightly to the left is the entrance to the Kızlar Ağası Hanı, or the Eunuch's Han. Be sure to take a look at the fountain to the left of the entrance.

KIZLAR AĞASI HANI (EUNUCH'S HAN)–3C
[kuhz-LAHR ah-ah-SUH hahn-UH]

The Eunuch's Han (Kızlar Ağası Hanı) was built in 1740 by Sultan Mahmut I's chief black eunuch, Beşir Ağa, who also built a mosque near Topkapı Palace. (As you probably know, eunuchs were castrated male slaves, considered "safe" to guard the harem.) Just to the left of the entrance is a lovely Ottoman fountain on which you can see the seal of the sultan on the upper section, with Ottoman poetry inscribed below.

There are some very unique shops in this han, particularly near the entrance. Take time to walk into the han's courtyard and look for signs of its original construction.

This han is another one where gold is melted and

Ottoman fountain outside han (above), inner courtyard collonade (below).

poured into molds, then pressed into thin ribbons or pulled into wire, as you may have seen in the İmam Ali Han. Notice the grilles on the floor to catch the gold dust, which is swept into sacks weekly and saved until there is enough to burn off the dust and recover the precious metal.

> As you exit the Eunuch's Han, take a left and follow the street (Tığcılar Sokak) until you reach a sign on the right for the Rococo Center.

MERCAN ALİ PAŞA HAN (ROCOCO CENTER)–4C
[mayr-JAHN ah-LEE pah-SHAH hahn]

This han, which was once quite charming, has been remodeled into a modern shopping mall. The former Mercan Ali Paşa Han was where *kilim*s and rugs were washed with soap and water. They were then spin-dried and laid flat on the roof to finish drying in the sun; when the weather was bad, the rugs and *kilim*s were hung in a warm room to dry.

This is an excellent example of how modernization is eliminating much of the charm of old Istanbul. Of course, the trade done in this new jewelry mall is far more profitable than the cleaning of rugs, so although the fascinating old ways have been cast aside, these shops will certainly contribute more to the Turkish economy.

Continue along the same road (Tığcılar Sokak) until you reach the T-intersection with Mercan Caddesi, where you will take a right. The very old han you see first on your right is the Büyük Ticaret Han, and beyond that on your right across the first street is the Küçük Yeni Han.

KÜÇÜK YENİ HAN–5C
[kew-CHEWK yay-NEE hahn]

The Küçük Yeni Han (small new han) was built in the 18th century by Sultan Mustafa III. It's a very large han, but it got its name in comparison to its sizable neighbors, the Büyük Yeni Han (big new han) and the Büyük Valide Han (big mother's han). This han has a unique charm with its small mosque and minaret perched on the roof. The mosque, which you may only be able to see from across the street, resembles a Byzantine church, a style common hundreds of years previous to its construction.

The upper windows of the han are many-paned arches, while the lower windows have heavy square marble frames with iron grates. On the north façade of the building along Mercan Caddesi there are a few birdhouses, and a small fountain decorates the corner below the mosque, but sadly, it has been more recently used for heaping trash.

Continue along down the same street (now Çakmakçılar Yokuşu), crossing the street to the next han on your right, the Büyük Yeni Han.

BÜYÜK YENİ HAN–6c
[bew-YEWK yay-NEE hahn]

Look up at the eaves on the corner of the building to see a birdhouse built into the side of this ancient building. The Ottomans believed birds to be semi-sacred, as they considered them halfway between earth and heaven, so they often added birdhouses to the façades of their buildings. Many of them are surprisingly ornate, as this one obviously was.

As you look down the street, you can see that this han was built with angled corners on each room so that people on the upper story could observe activity along the street without hanging out the windows. This was a typical feature of Ottoman architecture, usu-ally intended for women, who were often sequestered in upper-story rooms (harems).

Turn right at this corner (Sandalyeciler Sokak) and walk up the street until you come to the entrance to this huge han on your left.

A barely noticeable birdhouse decorates the wall to the left of the street gate to the Büyük Yeni Han. Step inside and walk along to the archway on your left. You will enter the han through a second gate, the mammoth upper gate, which brings you to the third story of the han.

This han was built in 1764 by Sultan Mustafa III and because it

was one of the newer hans in Istanbul at that time, it earned the name Büyük Yeni Han (*büyük* means big, and *yeni* means new). It was second in size only to the Büyük Valide Han across the street, which you will visit later on this walk. Interestingly, because this han is built on a steep hill, each of its three stories is at street level on one side of the building, although only the ground floor and third story have gates to the street. None of the shops on the streets outside of the han have access to the courtyard, which is securely barricaded at night and on Sunday. There is a small postern gate within the main gate of the lower entrance, which is used by the porter and his family when the han is closed.

The angled corners of the Büyük Yeni Han along Çakmakçılar Yokuşu.

From this upper gallery you can see half of the narrow courtyard below. The courtyard was the longest one in the city — 100 meters, about the length of a football field — but has unfortunately been divided in the middle by a later construction. If you walk along the corridor, you will pass the barrier to see the other side of the han, helping you envision the huge gallery that was once actually more like an arena than a han. You can still see the original construction of the archways and along the corridors you will see that many shopkeepers have constructed overhead storage space within the arched ceilings.

As you can see, much of this han is devoted to silver crafting, though it is slowly being converted to textiles, as are many of the hans and shops in Istanbul.

As you leave the han, turn left to continue up Sandalyeciler Sokak. Walk past the first left turn and just beyond it enter an open passage on your left called Abut Efendi Han. This is the "back door" to the Yenni Tcharchi Han.

STAMBOUL YENNI-TCHARCHI HAN–7C
[stahm-BOOL yay-NEE chahr-SHUH hahn]

The modern interior of this han has many shops with children's clothing, particularly the elegant sultan-like outfits for young boys' circumcision celebrations. When you are halfway down the corridor, turn to admire a unique clock behind you up under the glass roof. Above a stag's head you will see a clock much like Western clocks but with Ottoman (Arabic) numerals in its face. Unfortunately, the clock no longer keeps time—its hands are no longer with us.

As you step back onto the street at the far end of the corridor, look above the entrance. The Turkish name Yeni Çarşı, which means "new market," is written with its French spelling, *Stamboul Yenni Tcharchi*, as well as in Ottoman script. This way foreigners, who could not read Ottoman, would still be able to pronounce the name of this han. Many Ottoman merchants and architects traveled to Europe towards the end of the 19th century and they returned eager to westernize their city.

Note the name in both Roman and Ottoman script (above) and the Ottoman clock face under the glass roo (left).

The Greek term "Stin-boli" meant "to/in the city," and it is believed that Stamboul was a variant of that term, which was in use for Constantinople during the Ottoman Empire. Obviously, this was the precursor to the modern name of Istanbul. The residents of this city have been called "Stamboullu" for centuries, although the city was not officially called Istanbul until the 1930s, well after the Turkish Republic was established.

The dual titles on this han's entry are clear evidence that the people of Istanbul welcomed westerners to their city. You will also see the date on both sides of the entryway. The *hegira* (Islamic lunar calendar) year 1313, on the right, corresponds to our calendar year 1895, on the left. As there was no need for stables or courtyards so late in the Ottoman era, this han's central corridor is just that—a passageway.

Look across the street and you will see the Yarım Han ("half han"). This han is divided in two, and the other half faces another street (Bezciler Sokak). It's a lovely building and its Art Deco façade indicates that it, too, was built in the early 1900s, so of course it wouldn't have a courtyard or stables.

Turn left as you leave the han and walk down Mahmut Paşa Yokuşu, passing two intersections on your left and four on your right. On your left you will come to a long building with an ancient upper story with zigzag brick designs under the eaves (corbels).
This is the Kürkçü Han.

KÜRKÇÜ HAN–8C
[kewrk-CHEW hahn]

Through the arched gateway is the ancient Kürkçü Han, the han of the furriers. Not long ago it was a paradise for knitters, with all types and colors of yarn, but that, too, has changed. Today few furriers remain; the majority of the han's trade is in textiles, featuring mainly bath and bed linens and clothing.

The Kürkçü Han is said to be the oldest surviving Ottoman han in the city, though little of the original han remains. It was built in the 15th century by Mahmut Paşa, Sultan Mehmet the Conqueror's famous Grand Vizier. He was of Byzantine origin, descending from one of the leading aristocratic families. He served as a general under the last Byzantine Emperor, Constantine XI Dragases and his grandfather

Philaninos governed in Greece.

This ancient han originally consisted of two huge courtyards. One had about 45 rooms arranged around a small mosque, which has been replaced by an apartment building (no feast for the eyes). The second was smaller and quite irregular, but it is now in ruins. The ancient wall you see beyond the han is the side wall of the Büyük Yeni Han.

Go left as you leave the Kürkçü Han and walk down to Çakmakçılar Yokuşu, a busy intersection. Take a sharp left and walk up the hill. Pass the first cross street on your right, and just beyond it on your right is the Sümbüllü Han.

SÜMBÜLLÜ HAN–9C
[sewm-bewl-LEW hahn]

Ottoman fountain in
Sümbüllü Han courtyard.

quakes, but because
of this combined
construction they
remain more or less
intact and upright.

Apart from the
Sümbüllü Han's
entrance, which
dates back to the 18th
century, most of the
han has been rebuilt.
The cloth dealers
here are wholesalers,
supplying goods to shops in and
around the Grand Bazaar and
across Anatolia. Note the vegetation growing from the walls of
the Büyük Valide Han next door.

The courtyard of the Sümbüllü
Han offers a great view of the
ancient eastern façade of the
famous Büyük Valide Han, your
next stop. Note the combined
stone and brick construction, a
technique used by the Byzantines
to prevent damage during earthquakes. A massive stone building
may be very sturdy, but it can easily collapse during an earthquake,
while the softer material of brick
helps to absorb some of the shock.
There are still city walls dating
back to the 4th and 5th centuries
which may rock during earth-

Turn right when you exit
the Sümbüllü Han and
continue up the street
until you come to the huge
gate of the Büyük Valide Han,
with its entrance at the intersection of the cross street.

BÜYÜK VALİDE HAN–10C
[bew-YEWK vah-lee-DAY hahn]

Valide (also *valde*) means mother. This han was commissioned in 1651 by Kösem Sultan, the mother of two sultans, Sultan Murat IV and his successor Sultan İbrahim. However, it was not built until the reign of her grandson, Sultan Mehmet IV. Except for a few wives of reigning sultans, the mothers of sultans were the most influential women in the Ottoman Empire. (The title Sultan comes *before* the name when it is a man, as in Sultan Mehmet, and *after* the name when it is a woman: Kösem Sultan.)

Note the massive doors as you enter the first courtyard. These huge iron-plated wooden doors are still used to secure the han at night and on Sundays for the safety of both residents and merchandise. If you come on a Sunday, they will be closed and padlocked. The small wicket door built into of one of the gate wings was used for travelers who came after sundown when it was still used as an inn; now it is used by the keeper and his family when the han is closed. There is a set of these doors between each of the three courtyards of this han.

This is the largest han in Istanbul—the only one with three intact courtyards (the central one is the largest). Although it is in poor condition, the Büyük Valide Han evokes a clear idea of the type of lodgings available to cara-

Büyük Valide Han

vans along the famed Silk Road. The typical construction of colonnaded galleries allowed for shade, privacy, and ventilation, as well as an ability to oversee courtyard activity from above. As you explore this han, try to imagine it as a new structure bustling with merchants from across Asia Minor and beyond.

The first courtyard is irregularly shaped, mainly to conform to the surrounding streets.

There is a stairway leading up to the second level in the archway between the first and second courtyards. Walk up the stairs and continue to your right. You'll see a few deserted storefronts almost like homes, complete with front doors and ornately grated windows. Further down on your left is a shiny glass door, which is the han's takeaway restaurant. Open the door and ask for Mehdi Bey, a retired weaver who will let you up on the roof. Though he doesn't speak much English, he will understand. Please tip him for this service.

Notice the mosque in the central courtyard, one of very few han mosques that still survives. It has no minaret and no dome, as it was originally built for Shiites, although it is now mainly used by Sunnis. The majority of Turks are Sunni Muslims, but as this han was originally used by Persians living in Istanbul, it had a Shiite mosque. The Shiite denomination of Islam venerates the Prophet's cousin and son-in-law, Ali, and his two sons, Hasan and Hüseyin, the

Büyük Valide Han entrance on Sunday.

grandsons of the Prophet Mohammed. Every year on the 23rd day of the month of Muharrem, worshippers commemorated Hüseyin's martyrdom in Karbala in 638 with a procession down the street towards Eminönü, stripped to the waist, whipping and beating their backs with chains as the blood ran down their backs. Atatürk abolished such practices in the first years of the Turkish Republic.

Much of the han is deserted, but it is worth wandering the crumbling passageways to get a

"Antiques" destined for the Grand Bazaar (above), and detail of the "wicket" door for after-hours access to the han.

some of the huge spools lying around in the gallery.

There is an antique shop on the second level, where Serkan Özcan sells "antiques" that he makes for shops in the bazaar. If the door is closed, ring the buzzer and he'll come down from his upstairs workshop, which you can also see if you wish.

feel for the life that once existed there. Only a few of the original 54 weaving looms still operated in this han when weaving here was finally forbidden in 2007. Most of the looms were 60 to 70 years old and their vibrations were such a problem that they were shut down. You may see

The Büyük Valide Han's roof offers an amazing panoramic view of Istanbul. Climbing the crumbling narrow stairway is an adventure in itself, well worth the breathtaking view from the many-domed roof of this venerable han. If you don't get up there, never fear. You'll have an opportunity for a similar view from the top of the Sair Han, this han's third courtyard, later on this tour.

➡ " See profile of antique whole-saler Serkan Özcan on page 134."

➡ " See profile of weaver Mehdi Çardak on page 135."

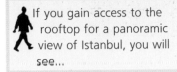

If you gain access to the rooftop for a panoramic view of Istanbul, you will see...

THE TOWER OF EIRENE–11C

From the roof of the Valide Han you can see the Tower of Eirene just adjacent to the han. Dating back to the Byzantine period, it was once 27 meters high and at one time its top floor was used as a small mosque.

Unfortunately, it was partly destroyed in 1926 during an earthquake and is now used for storage. It is a square, truncated tower of brick and stone layers, its top overgrown with grass and mosses.

Exit the Büyük Valide Han where you entered and take a right on the Çakmakçılar Yokuşu. Follow that straight to the intersection at the top of the hill and turn right. The Hıdiv Han is the large white building about a half block down on your right (#16) with a brilliant red sign over the door. Look above the door for the inscription.

HİDİV HAN–12C
[huh-DEEV hahn]

This han was financed by Halim Paşa, the son of Hıdiv (Khedive) Ali Paşa, the Viceroy of Egypt. It was built in the classical style popular in the early 1900s. Over the door is an inscription which in English means:

> *"This han was donated to the Red Crescent on April 17, 1930, by the deceased Lady Tarendil, the wife of Halim Paşa, who was the son of Hıdiv Mehmet Ali Paşa."*

In other words, the han was donated to the Red Crescent, the Islamic equivalent of the Red Cross, by the daughter-in-law of Mehmet Ali Paşa, who ruled Egypt as an Ottoman governor. The Hıdiv Han's four stories house boutiques and workshops, primarily involved in the import, manufacture, and sale of textiles.

Continue down Uzunçarşı Caddesi a few more blocks until you see an ancient han on your left. Incidentally, this street was once called Macros Embolos, the Byzantine market street that was the major route from the Forum of Constantine to the Golden Horn. Though the name of this important street has changed from Greek to Turkish, its translation in both languages is "the long market."

KİLİT HAN—13C
[kee-LEET hahn]

Kilit Han is one of the oldest buildings in this area. Its lower part is Byzantine, dating to the fifth century, while its upper part is Ottoman, built in the 17th century. Notice the round arches of the lower section, while the Ottoman arches are pointed. This han was constructed in a rectangle, though its parallel sides are unequal. An entry was added on the upper story to gain access to the rooftop and a view of the street, although it is not open to the public.

Although only a small part of the han appears old from the street (much of the façade has been plastered and painted over), take a sharp turn to your left as soon as the building ends. It will take you up Nargileci Sokak, from which you can see a lovely view of the ancient side of the han fronted by a small park.

According to some sources, a lovely palace, the Çift Saray, was situated just up the hill from this han. Sadly, it was destroyed by fire at the turn of the century. The side view of the han helps us imagine the scene of this picturesque han surrounded by beautiful palace gardens.

Continue down Uzunçarşı Caddesi another block until you see a small mosque on the left-hand corner.

BEZZAZ-I CEDİD CAMİSİ (MOSQUE)–14C
[bay-zahz-UH jay-DEED JAH-mee-see]

This mosque dates back to the 16th century. The rectangular white stones on the minaret indicate the staircase leading to the little balcony, which is decorated with zigzag bricks. Step around the corner to see the best view of this quaint mosque, which was renovated in 1990.

> Continue down Uzunçarşı Caddesi another half block to the first right turn past the mosque. This small street will lead you to a mosque situated in a V between two roads.

ÇANDARLIZADE ATİK İBRAHİM ALİ PAŞA CAMİSİ (MOSQUE)–15C
[chahn-dahr-luh-zah-DAY ah-TEEK ee-brah-HEEM ah-LEE pah-SHAH JAH-mee-see]

Peer through the archway to view this mosque, which is over 500 years old. Completed in 1478 by Çandarlı İbrahim Paşa, Grand Vizier under Sultan Beyazıt II, it is one of the oldest mosques in the city. Its most notable feature is the ornate parapet on its minaret but, unfortunately, most of its original structure was lost in a recent renovation.

> If you take the right-hand road above the mosque, it will lead you into the a parking lot just outside the Sair Han. Cross the parking lot to the far corner, where the building looks the oldest. There is an entry in the corner below an outside stairway that leads to an upper level.

SAİR HAN (SAĞIR HAN)–16C
[sah-EER hahn]

The history of this han is vague at best. It is actually the third courtyard of the neighboring Büyük Valide Han. The only documentation available about the date of construction was a marble plaque (now gone) located in a passage between the Sair Han and the Büyük Valide Han. It indicated that in 1651, Sultan Ahmet I's wife, Kösem Sultan (who had been brought from Crete), had this han built during her grandson's reign, long after her husband's death.

When you step into the han you will see a courtyard below you, which was primarily used to stable the horses of travelers. For a short time it was used to raise fighting cocks, which has since been forbidden. A rough stairway leads down into the courtyard, but you should probably stay on the upper level. Walk along to your right and look across the courtyard. The crumbling brick building that sits atop the northeast corner of this han is the Tower of

Sair Han rooftop view overlooking Istanbul.

A man named Apkar, an Armenian from Sivas, established his printing press on this site in the 16th century after traveling to Venice to get type in Armenian script. This was not the first printing press in the city, since Jews fleeing the Spanish Inquisition had brought in Hebrew type at the end of the 15th century.

Step back outside the han and if you have the energy, climb the stairway along the right-hand (east) wall to a rooftop terrace. Though the roof has become a haven for stray dogs, the view of the Sea of Marmara from here is spectacular and you will also have a close-up view of the Tower of Eirene at the far end of the rooftop. Additionally, there is one of a very few original chimneys from the han. It's well worth the effort, particularly if you didn't get to the roof of the Büyük Valide Han.

Eirene, a Byzantine structure over a thousand years old (see the Büyük Valide Han).

As it was inhabited mainly by Persians, the Ottomans called this han the Han of the Foreigners or Sair Han (*sair* = others). The shield on the "Sair Han" was refurbished during a later restoration and the name changed to "Sağır," which means deaf, perhaps because of the deafening noise of the 54 weaving mills working there.

At the bottom of the outdoor stairway to the upper terrace, follow the road down to your right around the building, turning left to follow it as it goes along the lower wall of the mosque. You will see a small road leading down the hill to your right, which you will take down to Vasıf Çınar Caddesi. Note the beautiful decoration on the corner of the building to your right. This is the Amerikan Han.

AMERİKAN HAN–17C
The American Bible House

The handsome neoclassical Amerikan Han was built by an American missionary named Isaac Bliss in the 1880s. His goal was to serve the Christian community in Turkey. The Bible Society Office and the American Board were housed there, along with a small church, the Emmanuel Protestant Church.

The American Board Publication Department had offices in the building complex as well. The department was named the Redhouse Press in 1966 in honor of Sir James Redhouse, who wrote the famous Redhouse Turkish-English dictionaries between 1861 and 1890.

There were many Americans working in this building complex at that time, primarily because the area had been the center of publishing houses in Istanbul. Over the years, most Americans migrated across the Golden Horn. Consequently, the chapel in the complex has most recently been used by Protestant Armenians and Syriac Christians (from Southeast Turkey). In 1996 the han was handed over to SEV (Health and Education Foundation), a private Turkish philanthropic foundation, which still publishes the Redhouse Dictionaries through its publishing arm in Üsküdar. The building is gradually being closed down.

Continue to your right, following the same street (Vasıf Çınar Caddesi) slightly downhill. Notice the beautiful decorations on the corner building, which is now Garanti Bank. Walk one more block to the next intersection, where you will turn right on M.R. Alaca Hamam Sokak. About a half block up on your right you will come to the Büyük Çorapçı Han.

BÜYÜK ÇORAPÇI HAN–18C
[bew-YEWK chohr-ahp-CHUH hahn]

The Büyük Çorapçı Han was built in the 16th century by Piyale Paşa, Sultan Süleyman's Grand Admiral. Though it was not a large han, it was important because of its proximity to the Egyptian Bazaar. Since the main commerce of the han was the making and selling of socks, it was named the Büyük Çorapçı (big stocking merchant) Han. In the early 1900s, two of the rooms on the second floor were joined and converted into a small synagogue for the Jewish merchants of this area, while a second pair of rooms was converted into a prayer room for Muslims.

Büyük Çorapçı
Han
courtyard view
(above), and
street entrance
(right).

Turn left as you leave the Büyük Çorapçı Han and walk to the corner. Turn left back onto Vasıf Çınar Caddesi and go one block. Turn right onto Sabuncu Han Sokak. The Leblebici Han is the old building on your right near the corner.

LEBLEBİCİ HAN–19C
[lay-blay-bee-JEE hahn]

According to legend, this han, which dates back to the 16th century, was built by Roxelana (Hürrem Sultan). She was a Russian slave chosen from the harem by Süleyman the Magnificent, who later broke tradition to wed her. It is doubtless one of the oldest of the hans behind the Egyptian (Spice) Bazaar. Look up to admire its charming little second story. It was once a market for the roasting and selling of chickpeas, a favorite food in Turkey to this day (*leblebi* means "roasted chickpeas").

Leblebici Han exterior (above) and courtyard arched collonade (below).

Continue down the street less than a half block and you will see the modern entry to the Marpuççular Çarşısı on your right.

MARPUÇÇULAR ÇARŞISI–20C
[mahr-pooch-choo-LAHR char-shuh-SUH]

The word *marpuç* means the mouthpiece of a water pipe, so it is clear that this han dealt in the trade of *nargiles* or water pipes. Unfortunately, the old han was recently torn down and rebuilt. The most notable thing about it today is that it still houses a small mosque on the second story to the left of the stairway. You may step inside if you take off your shoes and are appropriately covered.

Most of the merchants in this han now sell beads for jewelry and clothing (wholesale, although you may purchase them as well).

Second-story mosque inside Marpuççular Çarşısı.

 Turn right as you exit the Marpuççular Çarşısı and continue down Sabuncu Han Sokağı, crossing the next street. Halfway down the next block on your right is what is left of the Sabuncu Han.

SABUNCU HAN–21C
[sah-boon-JOO hahn]

Entrance to toy-filled Sabuncu Han.

Located directly behind the Egyptian Bazaar, this han was built in the 19th century. *Sabun* means soap in Turkish, and at that time soap was brought here to sell. Cleanliness has always been an important part of Muslim culture, as can be seen by the popularity of the *hamam*, the Turkish bath. This was obviously an important han, since the street has taken its name. At one time it had a small courtyard and a second, larger, colonnaded courtyard where merchants from the area kept their horses. Unfortunately, most of it was recently destroyed in a fire. Today in the Sabuncu Han you will find wholesalers of spices, toys, perfumes, Christmas tree trimmings, and stationery goods, all at very reasonable prices. Quite a change from soap, don't you think?

Continue down Sabuncu Han Sokak a half block to find the famous Spice Bazaar, better known in Istanbul as the Egyptian Market (Mısır Çarşısı).

MISIR ÇARŞISI
(EGYPTIAN MARKET/SPICE BAZAAR)–22C
[muh-SUHR chahr-shuh-SUH]

The Egyptian Bazaar was built in 1663 by Turhan Sultan, the mother of Sultan Mehmet IV, on the site of what was previously a Venetian market. It was part of the Yeni Cami (New Mosque) complex and it included 88 shops, selling all sorts of spices imported from Egypt (*Mısır*) and other areas in the East. You can still find different spices and herbs, as well as oils and roots that allegedly possess medicinal value. The Egyptian Bazaar also offers many other varieties of merchandise. Expect to be offered a sample of the famous *lokum* (Turkish delight) as you stroll past the shops.

On the second floor of the bazaar is a famous old restaurant called Pandeli,

which is only open for lunch. It's a bit pricey but it's famous for its fine cuisine. Although the bazaar is closed on Sundays, the outdoor

markets along each side of the building are always open. The side nearest the mosque sells gardening and pet supplies, as well as pets from parrots to monkeys—look also for the leeches used for medicinal purposes—while the western side of the building offers spices, cheese, dried fruit, fresh fruit, fish and other food items.

Be sure to watch your wallet around here; any crowded tourist area is bound to have pickpockets and this area is no exception.

Vaulted gallery of the Spice Bazaar (above) and one of its many spice displays (below).

BEDROS MURADYAN
Designs and creates molds for pressed metal impressions / Zincirli Han

Ohannes Muradyan was trained by an Austrian master and started the mold-making business in 1944. His son Bedros, once his apprentice, now continues the trade since his father's retirement. It is a precise craft, one that requires the careful engraving of two sides of a mold to fit closely together. The mold is first made from wood, then recrafted in

steel by chiseling the form into two heavy pieces that fit perfectly together, one concave and the other convex. To form the intended object (buttons, medals, pins, awards, coins, etc.), the two sides of the mold are pressed together with a piece of thin metal between them. (Muradyan's press creates 40 tons of pressure on the metal.) Once these steel molds are completed, they can be used repeatedly to press gold, brass, silver, copper or tin into the desired shape.

Bedros Bey pointed out how important it is to clean all the dust off the molds before pressing in order to make a perfect impression. This craft is one of the many dying arts of Istanbul, and Bedros Bey is one of a very few craftsmen in the world who still create these molds by hand.

As in most han workshops, Bedros Bey works six days a week, from 9 a.m. to 6 p.m. He is proud to work in the Zincirli Han, one of the loveliest of Istanbul's hans.

SERKAN ÖZCAN
Antique finisher and wholesaler / Büyük Valide Han

Though much of the Büyük Valide Han is now deserted and falling into disrepair, Serkan Özcan has maintained his antique shop on the second floor since 1993. His trade, which he learned from his father Salim, involves making "antiques" to be sold at the Grand Bazaar, as well as through a number of catalog outlets.

His shop is filled with hanging lanterns of every kind, as well as a wide variety of brass and metalware, made to look either new or antique, whatever suits your fancy. His upstairs workshop is unique; it has a domed ceiling so that when you stand in a certain spot, you hear your voice amplified. It is a strange sensation, and Serkan Bey takes great pleasure in letting his customers try it out. One day when he came to work he discovered that his roof and chimney were crumbling, so he had to incorporate his workshop into his downstairs showroom until they could be repaired. Serkan Bey works from 9 a.m. to 6 p.m. six days a week, as do most other han artisans. His wares are sold in the Grand Bazaar and shops in Antalya as well as through his catalog.

If you ask kindly, he will find the caretaker of the Büyük Valide

Han to open the door to the roof for you. (If you are so lucky, be sure to tip both of them a few lira for their efforts.) The view from the roof of this han is incredible—well worth the trip. Even the climb up the winding staircase beyond the ancient wooden door is an adventure. Walk to the far end of the roof and snap at least a hundred photos. If you time it right, you might even be treated to the concert of twenty simultaneous calls to prayer. It's truly amazing.

MEHDİ ÇARDAK
Weaver / Büyük Valide Han

The booming sound of fifty plus looms has subsided in the Büyük Valide Han, but retired weaver Mehdi Çardak says he continues to ply his trade (pardon the pun) for up to 13 hours a week. He has worked in his second-floor shop for 33 years and still owns two huge looms: a Belgian one made in 1953 and an Italian one made in 1948. He learned his trade by working beside a master for seven years before he could work on his own. Textile dealers would provide the yarn and the designs, and Mehdi Bey was paid for weaving *kilims*, scarves, and other textiles. Like other weavers, he maintained his own shop and was paid for the amount of weaving he completed.

Now that he is retired, his favorite pastime is sitting on the roof of the Büyük Valide Han enjoying the spectacular view of Istanbul, the Golden Horn, and the Sea of Marmara.

Antique etching of the Süleymaniye Mosque overlooking the Golden Horn.

Walk D
Sites above Eminönü

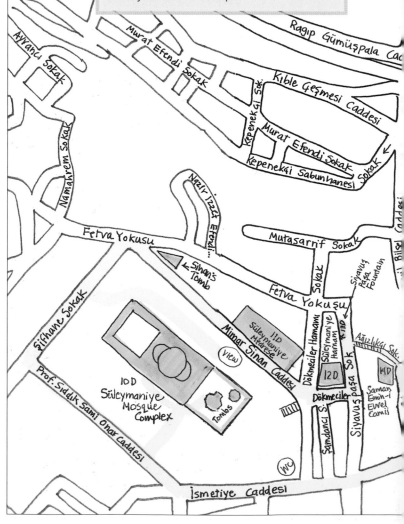

TO BEGIN WALK D:
Take the tram or the ferry to Eminönü, where you will walk under the street and up next to the Yeni Cami. The Spice Bazaar is the ancient stone and brick building behind the right-hand (west) courtyard of the mosque.

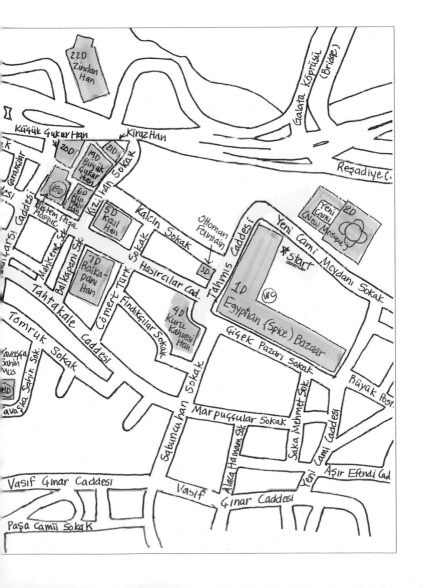

MISIR ÇARŞISI (EGYPTIAN MARKET / SPICE BAZAAR)–1D
[zeen-jeer-LEE hahn]

For a description of this site, flip back to page 130 at the end of Walk B.

🚶 Come out the front entrance of the Spice Bazaar. The mosque to your right, often teeming with activity, is the most prominent feature. You can enter the courtyard through any of the three entrances. Be sure to remove your shoes and be appropriately covered before entering the mosque.

YENİ CAMİ (NEW MOSQUE)–2D
[yay-NEE JAH-mee]

Despite its name, this mosque is not exactly new, although it has been recently restored to once again gleam at its post overlooking the Golden Horn. It was first commissioned in 1597 by Valide Safiye Sultan, the mother of Sultan Mehmet III. Unfortunately, when he died suddenly, she had to leave the palace

to make room for the next sultan's family. Consequently, the mosque remained unfinished and incurred significant damage until 1663, when it was completed, six sultans later, by the mother of Sultan Mehmet IV, Turhan Sultan. (Turhan Sultan also financed the Egyptian Bazaar.) Except for a few wives of reigning sultans, the mothers of sultans were the most influential women in the Ottoman Empire.

The New Mosque West stairway opens onto a courtyard in front of the Spice Bazaar.

Much like many imperial mosques, this mosque was designed similarly to the famous Hagia Sophia, with a central dome flanked by semidomes. The Yeni Cami has four semidomes rather than the Hagia Sophia's two, and it also has small domes at each corner. This creates a very pleasing cascading effect when you look up at the ceiling. The tiles are beautiful, though of lesser quality than in many other mosques in the city.

A colonnaded upper gallery surrounds the interior, a portion of which is screened off by a gilded metal grille that was for the sultan and his male family members. The sultan gained access to this Imperial Loge through a ramp located behind the mosque. His private quarters also include a salon, a bedroom, and a toilet, as well as kitchens on the lower level.

Generally, a mosque was the focal point for a *külliye*, a complex of buildings around the mosque. The Yeni Cami complex included a hospital, a medrese, two public fountains, a mausoleum, and a market, which financially supported the *külliye*'s institutions. The market of the Yeni Cami is obviously the Egyptian Bazaar, which has survived far longer than the school, hospital and public bath.

As you leave the mosque, walk past the front entrance to the Spice Bazaar, turn left and follow the right side of the building. There are cheese and spice stands along the way. Just as you get to the first buildings on the right, stop and look at the marble fountain in the wall.

OTTOMAN FOUNTAIN–3D

This lovely Ottoman fountain features elegant script above the fountain as well as elegant marble decorations, surrounded by classical columns carved into the wall. The Ottomans considered it an important service to provide drinking water for the public, and this fountain was surely funded by someone eager to "pave" his or her way to heaven through this generous gesture.

 Continue up the street to the end where it turns to the left, and you will see a tall white building wrapped around the street corner.

KURU KAHVECİ HAN—4D
[koo-ROO kah-vay-JEE hahn]

*For general information on hans,
see the introduction and the
text box on page 30.*

Façade of Kuru Kahveci Han.

The Kuru Kahveci Han was built in 1912, long after there was a need for stables or a courtyard. Instead, the downstairs rooms were let as shops or workshops and the upstairs ones were used as offices. It was designed by an architect named Zühtü for Mehmet Efendi, a coffee dealer. The name of the building and the date are written over the entrance in both Ottoman and the French spelling, *Kourou Kahvedji*, evidence of the city's eagerness to welcome Europeans. Notice how striking this concave façade is with its unique combination of floral and geometric design. The gate and the interior stairway emulate the Art Deco style, while the exterior of the building incorporates both Art Deco and classical design elements. If you step inside, you'll see the "lift," a box on a rope used to carry cups of coffee and tea up through the center of the once elegant spiral staircase to merchants and businessmen on the upper floors.

Mehmet Efendi was once the city's most famous coffee importer and there was always a line of people outside the han waiting to purchase coffee. Now the queue has moved to a newer storefront around the corner, where the air is always filled with the tantalizing aroma of fresh-ground coffee. Today the businesses in the Kuru Kahveci Han deal in a variety of items other than coffee.

> Turn and walk back down the street to the first left turn (Hasırcılar Caddesi) and follow it down a few blocks to Kızılhan Sokak (Balkapanı Sokak goes to the left), which is the first street that crosses from both sides. (It's the street of Christmas trimmings.) Turn right and walk a half block down to the entrance to the Kızıl Han, which is an ancient archway on your right, directly across from another archway on your left.

KIZIL HAN (PAPAZ HAN)–5D
[kuh-ZUHL hahn]

This han was built by the son of a priest (*papaz*) in the 16th century and is therefore also known as Papaz Han. Its massive entrance and construction are remarkable, though its interior is crumbling in disrepair. The outside wall faces the Golden Horn and presents an impressive reminder of the ancient history of this area. The Byzantine style of construction with a combination of stone and brick held stronger through earthquakes than earlier stone-only construction techniques. In the past the south façade was hidden behind city walls, but they were destroyed in 1980, so this ancient han fronts on the open parking area of Eminönü. The open courtyard within the han has been built up with shops and storage buildings and most of the cells around the courtyard are used only for storage. Note the Ottoman peaked archways along the colonnaded galleries. One can only hope that funding will be found to restore this decaying building.

> Directly across from the entrance to the Papaz Han is the Burmalı Han. Step across the street and through the passage into the next courtyard.

BURMALI HAN (HURMALI HAN)–6D
[BOOR-mah-luh hahn]

This ancient han from the early Byzantine era dates back to the sixth or seventh century, as evidenced by its round arches. There is some controversy over its name, as most sources call it the Burmalı Han (*burma* in Turkish means "twisting"), while others call it Hurmalı Han, since *hurma* in Turkish means "dates." Who knows?

Only part of the original han remains. It has a long, narrow courtyard, one side of which is the eastern façade of Rüstem Paşa Mosque, and the narrow passageway that leads towards the water is lined with spice wholesalers. (You will see these hans, the Büyük Çukur and Küçük Çukur Hans, at the end of this walk.) Climb to the second floor to see an example of the domed, vaulted ceilings, made with bricks in a herringbone pattern like those in the Basilica Cistern, that were typical at that time. It's hard to imagine the process that was used to construct these domes. As in the Papaz Han, these upstairs rooms are used for storage.

This han was used as a court of law in the 16th century, hence the name of a nearby street, Mahkeme (law court or trial) Sokak.

Details of Byzantine archways and brickwork of the Burmalı Han.

➡ " See profile of sack seller Mehmet Bayalı on page 165."

Turn right as you exit the han (where you came in). The road name changes from Kızılhan Sokak to Balkapanı Sokak when you cross Hasırcılar Caddesi. Continue another half block to an archway on your left labeled Balkapanı Han No. 13.

BALKAPANI HAN–7D
[BAHL-kah-pah-nuh hahn]

Balkapanı is probably the oldest han in Istanbul, and its name indicates that it was dedicated to the storage and sale of honey (*bal* = honey and *kapan* = market). Dating back to the forth or fifth century, it is, of course, Byzantine. Note the round Byzantine arches of the ground floor, compared to the pointed ones upstairs, which were added by the Ottomans. Venetians lived in this area before the Ottoman conquest in the 15th century, after which Ottomans moved in.

Its basement is immense, measuring 2000 square meters, with its entrance through a building located in the huge courtyard. It is fascinating—though unfortunately forbidden—to go downstairs and see the massive brick vaulting, supported by great rectangular pillars. With its vaulted ceilings similar to those you saw upstairs in the Burmalı Han, it feels a bit like the centuries-old wine cellars beneath French castles. Though most assume that this underground storehouse was a granary, some sources indicate that it may have held spices for the Venetians and honey for the Ottomans. Perhaps both are true. Today it is used to store cases of various goods for area merchants, and the manager keeps meticulous records of which vaults hold which merchandise.

When you exit the han, turn left and walk to the corner, where you will turn right onto Tahtakale Caddesi. Follow that a few blocks to busy Uzunçarşı Caddesi, the first cross street, the name of which means "the long market."

YAVAŞCA ŞAHİN CAMİSİ (KAPTAN PAŞA MOSQUE)–8D
[yah-VAHSH-chah shah-HEEN JAH-mee-see]

This was once the main route from the Golden Horn up to the Forum of Constantine on the second hill. During Byzantine times this street was lined with marble columns and was the main market street of the city.

Turn left on Uzunçarşı and walk up two blocks until you see a small mosque on your left.

This little mosque, Yavaşça Şahin or Kaptan Paşa Mosque, was built in the 15th century by Sultan Mehmet II's fleet captain. He was captain at the time of the Ottoman conquest, and he built this mosque shortly afterwards. Unfortunately, it was badly damaged in 1908 by a fire, but it has since been beautifully restored. The dome is perched on an octagonal structure, which is camouflaged by exterior walls beneath it. Notice the zigzag brick designs under the *şerefe* (minaret balcony) as well as under the eaves of the building. You will see this feature on many Ottoman buildings, particularly hans and mosques built before 1800.

> Directly across the street on your right is a parking ramp that was once an Ottoman open-air theater.

OPEN-AIR THEATER (destroyed)–9D

The other side of the street was once an open-air theater used by actors who performed in the center, while the spectators sat around them on the floor. This area is called Tahtakale, which means "wooden tower." At one time most of the shops in the area specialized in selling articles made of wood.

➡ " See profile of street cobbler Turan Görgör on page 166."

Continue along Uzunçarşı Caddesi to the second right turn, İsmetiye Caddesi. Every day but Sunday, you'll see an outdoor cobbler situated with his sewing machine and his shoemaker's last (foot-shaped mold) on the inside corner near a huge tree. Turn right at this corner and follow this street uphill. The main crossing is Siyavuşpaşa, and if you look to your right on the first street after you cross it (Şamdancı Sokak), you'll see a nice view of the Süleymaniye Hamamı, which you'll visit later. Continue straight up the cobbled street along a huge stone wall that was once the wall to the sultan's palace, the Eski Saray. Soon on your right you'll see the great Süleymaniye Mosque. The huge neoclassical gate you pass on your left near the mosque is a gate to Istanbul University, usually closed. You will come out onto an open cobbled street with restaurants on your left, probably the city's best restaurants for *kuru fasulye*, a Turkish bean dish. Walk along this street until you come to an entry to the mosque courtyard on your right.

SÜLEYMANİYE CAMİSİ (SÜLEYMANİYE MOSQUE)–10D
[sew-lay-MAH-nee-yay JAH-mee-see]

Overlooking the Golden Horn (Haliç) from Istanbul's third hill, the Süleymaniye Camisi dominates the skyline and is unquestionably the most magnificent mosque in the city. It is the largest of the 81 mosques designed by Turkey's greatest Ottoman architect, Sinan, who also built about 50 *mescit* (small mosques) as well as the grandest mosque in Turkey, the Selimiye Mosque in Edirne. Sinan didn't become the sultan's architect until his late fifties and he lived to be nearly 100. An incredibly prolific architect, he masterminded 321 buildings (mosques, schools, baths, etc.) in those 50 years, many of which were stupendous undertakings.

North façade of the Süleymaniye Mosque (left) and the east view from the inner courtyard (right).

Sinan designed this mosque for Sultan Süleyman the Magnificent, reputed to be the greatest of the Ottoman sultans. The mosque was constructed between 1550 and 1557; it took three years just to lay the foundations for the expansive complex. The surrounding *külliye* took many more years to complete, and most of it is still intact. You'll surely find that wandering through this complex evokes the atmosphere of life five centuries ago in Istanbul.

The exterior of the mosque is impressive from every angle with its many domes, porticoed court-

The mosque interior (above) and a
view of its cascading domes (right).

yards, multiple fountains, ornate
carving, and striking combina-
tions of different shades of marble. The mosque's four minarets
denote that Sultan Süleyman was
the fourth Ottoman sultan to reign
in Istanbul; their ten balconies
indicate that he was the tenth sultan of the House of Osman. The
nearly square mosque interior is
expansive without second-story
galleries, adding to the impression of its vastness. Mammoth
columns support cascading domes
from the central dome of the
mosque.

*Step inside the mosque,
making sure to be appropriately
covered.*

The limestone in the walls was
quarried in Bakırköy and the marble came from the Island of
Marmara. The 2000 oil lamps
looked like stars at night, and
ostrich eggs were hung to attract
their soot, which was scraped off
to make ink for the sultan's calligraphers. The acoustics are impressive in this mosque; you can hear
quiet voices clearly from across
the room. The mosque's beautiful
inscriptions were done by the
most famous Ottoman calligrapher, Ahmet Karahisari, and his

pupil Hasan Çelebi. All in all, this mosque is incredible; you could spend days studying each of its many features.

The story of Sultan Suleyman is fascinating as well. He became sultan at the age of 25 and during his 46-year reign he conquered many lands and brought order and justice to all of them, bringing the Ottoman Empire to its peak. He had this mosque built after returning victorious from his Hungarian campaign. His life was colored by his love for his favorite concubine, Roxelana, a Russian slave whom he named Hürrem (the laughing one). She exerted incredible influence in both his life and politics, and she coerced him to marry her, breaking with tradition. (When Sultan Beyazıt was taken prisoner by Tamerlane in 1402 at the Battle of Ankara, his wife had endured insults and disrespect. Because of that, it was decided that sultans would not marry, in order to spare their wives—always slaves—a similar fate.)

After becoming Sultan Süleyman's wife, her official name was Haseki Hürrem, although her husband supposedly continued to call her Roxelana. After she had her own sons, she persuaded her husband that his heir Mustafa (by a previous concubine) was a threat to his throne. Believing her stories, Süleyman ordered his favorite son strangled by his servants. Roxelana's eldest son, Sultan Selim II, succeeded his father. Some sources imply that Sultan Selim II was less great than his father, though he did expand the empire Sultan Süleyman had left him, adding Cyprus as well as other lands.

Step back out onto the courtyard and enter the gate into the cemetery next to the mosque, where you will see the tombs of Süleyman and his wife.

You can see the tombs of Sultan Süleyman and Hürrem Sultan (Roxelana) in the walled garden and graveyard behind the mosque, both decorated in the finest İznik tiles. Sultan Süleyman's is ornately decorated with Ottoman script and multicolored bright floral tiles, while Roxelana's tomb is smaller, with tiles of a more feminine motif featuring branches of small cherry blossoms.

According to John Freely in his book *John Freely's Istanbul,* the Süleymaniye complex "includes four *medreses* [theological schools] and their preparatory school, a school for reading the Kuran, a school of sacred tradition, a primary school, a medical college, a hospital, an insane asylum, a public kitchen, a caravanserai, a market street, a public bath, and two tombs" (mentioned above). Most of these buildings are still standing, and many are open to the public. Sinan's tomb is also located just outside the walls of the mosque courtyard on the lowest side (north corner) in a V between Fetva Yokuşu Sokağı and Mimar Sinan Caddesi.

Step back out onto the cobbled street lined with restaurants, then follow it around to your right. As you turn the first corner, you'll see stairs leading down to a tea shop. As you continue along that street, you'll pass the public kitchen (now a posh restaurant) and numerous *medreses*. On your right is a gate into the mosque gardens. If the gate is open, go in and walk to your left around the mosque to see the lovely walkway behind it. You'll have a spectacular view of Istanbul with the *medrese* chimneys in the foreground—a great photo op.

SÜLEYMANİYE MEDRESESİ–11D
[sew-lay-MAH-nee-yay may-dray-say-see]

These picturesque *medrese*s are built to the west of the *hamam*, on the steep northern slope of the third hill. They consist of five stories of cells, interconnected by a maze of four flights of stairs to accommodate the slope. Although they are not open to the public, you will get a spectacular view of Istanbul and the Golden Horn from the courtyard walkway above them.

Retrace your steps back through the gate to the street and continue around to your right along the walls. Take a sharp right at the next corner onto the cobbled street, still following the wall. On your left is the tomb of Sinan, the great architect who built this mosque complex. Continue along this street until you see the sign for the Süleymaniye Hamamı on your left.

SÜLEYMANİYE HAMAMI–12D
[sew-lay-MAH-nee-yay hah-mah-MUH]

This is the *hamam* (public bath) of the Süleymaniye complex, also built by the great architect Sinan in the 16th century. At that time it was called the Metalworkers' Bath because of its proximity to the foundries of that time. Sinan's private cubicle is still preserved within the *hamam*. Süleyman the Magnificent reputedly visited the *hamam* when it opened and the cubicle he used was later set aside for elite theological scholars. Over the centuries, the *hamam* has been mainly used by students of the Islamic theological college, and it is now once again open to the public. It is well preserved and recently restored; only minor changes have been made to the inside. Some say it is the most elegant of Istanbul's *hamams*, and it is one of few co-ed *hamams*, so fam-

ilies and couples can bathe together. (It even offers bathing suit tops and shorts for women.)

The domes of the *hamam* have little glass bulbs to let in light, at the same time preventing anyone on the roof from looking in. *Hamams* are always domed so that condensation runs down the walls instead of falling from the ceiling onto the people sitting on the heated marble slab beneath the dome.

➡️ " See profile of *hamam* worker Ayhan Bulut on page 167."

As you follow the cobbled street past the *hamam*, make an immediate left onto Dökmeciler Sokak. This is a narrow street that becomes a stairway as you head down along the side of the *hamam*. At the bottom of the street it comes to a T on Siyavuşpaşa. Turn left, and about a block down on the left side of the street you will see another Ottoman fountain.

SİYAVUŞ PAŞA FOUNTAIN–13D
[see-yah-VOOSH pah-SHAH]

Siyavuş Paşa was a Grand Vizier to Sultan Murat III during the 16th century. The bas-relief sculpture on his marble fountain represents the Tree of Life (the cypress, pointing towards heaven) usually seen on tombstones. It's a good example of the many Ottoman fountains that provided water for the inhabitants of Istanbul, though it no longer dispenses water.

Directly across from the fountain is a marble stairway leading downhill. This is Ağızlıkçı Sokak, where you will see shops with toys and dolls. At the bottom of this street on the right corner is another ancient mosque.

SAMAN EMİN-İ EVVEL CAMİİ (SAMANVEREN MOSQUE)–14D
[sah-MAHN ay-meen-ee ay-VAYL JAH-mee]

This 15th-century mosque was financed by Sultan Mehmet II's Inspector of Straw, named Sinan Ağa. (*Saman* means straw, *emin* means trustworthy, and *evvel* means first, so he obviously saw himself as a highly reliable and trustworthy inspector.) Its unusual minaret has no balcony but, instead, pretty lunette windows through which the *müezzin* recited his call to prayer five times each day. The bricks at the base of the minaret create a unique leaf-like decoration, perhaps in keeping with the role of Sinan Ağa.

Continue on the walkway to your right below the mosque to the main road, then head straight down toward the Yavaşça Şahin Mosque until you reach the buildings on the left. Turn left onto the lower road just after a tiny triangular park that splits the roadway. This is Ord. Professor Cemil Bilsel Caddesi. Follow the sidewalk about a block downhill until you come to a wide stairway leading down to your right onto a lower road (Bestekâr Basri Kebapçıhane Sokak) and follow it. Straight ahead of you is the ancient Şeyh Davut Han, and as you turn right onto Bestekâr Basri Sokak, the Bozkurt Han is the building on your immediate right.

BOZKURT HAN–15D
[bohz-KOORT hahn]

The Bozkurt Han is hardly notable unless you look up above the awnings to see its ancient façade, again with pretty zigzag brick designs on its cor-

bels. This dates it back to the 15th or 16th century. Don't bother to step inside—there's nothing of interest there.

On your left along this same street (Bestekâr Basri Sokak) is another ancient building. When you reach the corner you will see a birdhouse high above you under the eaves. Turn left to find the entrance.

ŞEYH DAVUT HAN–16D
[shayh dah-VOOT hahn]

Şeyh Davut Han entrance shield (above) and birdhouse nestled beneath its eaves (right)

The ancient building on your left is the 15th-century Şeyh Davut Han. Above its entrance, an inscription on a round shield tells us it was restored in the 19th century. Notice the fig tree that grows beside the birdhouse on the left corner under the roof. During Ottoman times, birds were considered heavenly creatures, so architects often incorporated birdhouses into the design of their buildings, hoping for a bit of a boost to heaven through providing shelter for their feathered friends. This han now has many shops surrounding its small central courtyard.

Continue to the end of the street to the corner and take a left on Paçacı Sokak, following it to the end. Turn right at the corner, and at the end of this street (Deveoğlu Sokak) you will see a second-story mosque.

EL HAÇ TİMUR TAŞ CAMİSİ (MOSQUE)–17D
[el HAHCH tee-moor TAHSH JAH-mee-see]

This ancient mosque, also known as Timurtaş Camisi, was probably built in the mid-15th century during the reign of Sultan Mehmet the Conqueror (Fatih). Its construction is very similar to that of the Samanveren Camisi (Straw Inspector's Mosque); both are built over a vaulted ground floor. Recently restored, it is a fine example of the brick and stone construction of the early Ottoman era. The notable feature of this tiny mosque is its minaret; instead of a balcony, it has four grilled windows from which the *muezzin* calls the faithful to prayer, as in the Samanveren Mosque.

Turn right on Kantarcılar Caddesi. The huge building on your left was once a *hamam* and is now used as a market, the *Hamam* Çarşı. When the road comes to a T, take a left on the main street, Uzunçarşı Caddesi. (Look familiar? You've been here earlier on this walk.) At the first intersection (Hasırcılar Caddesi) you will see the lovely Rüstem Paşa Mosque straight ahead of you. On the corner in front of you is one of the mosque's three entrances, a stairway up to the second-story courtyard.

RÜSTEM PAŞA CAMİSİ (MOSQUE)–18D
[rews-TAYM pah-SHAH JAH-mee]

This stunning little mosque was built in 1561 by the great Sinan (who built the Süleymaniye Mosque and many others); it's certainly one of the most enchanting of his small mosques. It was commissioned by Rüstem Paşa, who was a Grand Vizier to Sultan Süleyman the Magnificent, as well as husband to his favorite daughter, Princess Mihrimah. It was built

over a complex of shops whose profits supported the mosque and its *külliye*.

The west side of the mosque features double carpeted porches with domed bays for prayer. This unique feature is used by many who must certainly enjoy the opportunity to pray at a mosque and still be outdoors.

The interior of the mosque is an octagon inscribed in a rectangle, its dome resting on four semidomes. Its most impressive feature, though, is its tiles—thousands of which adorn the walls and columns of the mosque. These multicolored tiles were brought from İznik during the height

Men pray inside Rüstem Paşa Mosque (above), close-up of ornate carving in its marble Müezzin *mahfili*, or pulpit (below), and details of hand-painted İznik tiles (bottom).

of its tile-making fame. Take time to wander through the mosque's interior to marvel at the quality, variety, and vivid color of these works of the finest ceramics artisans in history. Though this lovely mosque is less well known than the Blue Mosque, it's truly one of Istanbul's finest gems.

Exit the Rüstem Paşa Mosque through the side visitors' entrance (with the shoe racks), then take the corner stairway down to your right (the northwest corner). At the bottom of the stairs, take an immediate sharp right (before the tea garden) and enter the archway just beside the mosque's stairway entrance. You'll walk down a short passage, where men sell used clothing and sundries, along the north side of Rüstem Paşa Mosque. Turn left at the end of this passage, down an even narrower passage (Rüstem Paşa Sokağı) where you'll see bags of spices (except on Sunday).

BÜYÜK ÇUKUR HAN (RÜSTEM PAŞA HAN)–19D
[bew-YEWK choo-KOOR hahn]

The well-preserved han on your right is also called Rüstem Paşa Han. It was built in the 16th century and has separate doors leading to the stables and to the cells upstairs. From the upper-story gallery you can catch a glimpse of its lovely arched courtyard porticoes through an inner office. A row of small rooms has been added on the open side of the gallery, so that upstairs you are in a dark corridor with many doors on each side rather than on an open colonnade as in most hans.

There is a dome painted much like the inside of a mosque, perhaps used as a prayer room at one time, but most probably just because of its prior role as a part of the mosque complex.

Çukur means "lower than the street level"—the main floor cells of both hans are lower than street level. *Büyük* (large) refers to this

han being the larger of the two hans belonging to the same complex. For centuries the Büyük Çukur Han has served as a space for spice merchants who have ground spices in huge mills, stored the spices, and sold them to local merchants and shipped them across the globe. Though spices are no longer ground here, they are still shipped through these businesses.

> The han on your left, probably lined with tubs of spices from spice merchants, is the Küçük Çukur Han.

KÜÇÜK ÇUKUR HAN–20D
[kew-CHEWK choo-KOOR hahn]

This is the smaller cousin of the Büyük Çukur Han and was also built in the 16th century. They both belong to the Rüstem Paşa complex. The word *küçük* means small, as opposed to its *büyük* (big) cousin across the street. It has separate doors leading to what was once the stables and to the cells upstairs. The upper gallery is crammed with merchandise, as this han has become more a warehouse than a market. Walking along this street lined with bins and bags of spices is a sensory experience—a feast of both colors and smells.

➡ "See profile of spice dealer Ulvi Sercar Serçe on page 168."

> Turn right at the end of this street onto the main street along the Golden Horn. The building directly to your right is the Kiraz Han.

KİRAZ HAN–21D
[kee-RAHZ hahn]

Although its name indicates that it is the han of cherries (*kiraz* means cherry), this han was used for storing wine for quite some time. Built in the 16th century, part of its outside wall is said to have incorporated the original city fortifications, though much of it

has been destroyed to make room for roads and parking. The building has been restored and now houses the offices of a government organization called Tarihi Çevreyi Koruma Müdürlüğü (Directorate of Protection of the Historical Environment). Fitting, don't you think?

Look across the main street for Storks, the building along the water to the left of the bus terminal area. There is an ancient tower on the far side of the building, which you can best see from the Galata Bridge.

ZİNDAN HAN–22D
[zeen-DAHN hahn]

The area on the other side of the highway is called Zindan Kapısı, or Prison Gate (*zindan* means dungeon). The Zindan Han (now Storks) was built at the beginning of the 19th century, against an ancient defense tower of the city walls of Constantinople. The Byzantines used the tower as a dungeon, and the famed envoy of Harun al-Rashid, Cafer Baba, was imprisoned there. In fact, this is why the Ottomans kept this tower even though they demolished many others. Part of the han was reputedly used as a women's prison for some time during the Ottoman period.

Lately it was converted from an office building into a retail mall with different goods on each floor, including leather, copper, carpets, and jewelry. The tower stands as it has for centuries, though, overlooking the bustle of traffic near the Galata Bridge. Fortunately, some things never change.

Whew! You've finished this walk, and perhaps even all four. Kudos to you! You've experienced many of the rich sensations of historical Istanbul, and hopefully these new insights will further enhance your experience as you savor the adventures that await you.

MEHMET BAYALI
Sack Seller / Burmalı Han

Mehmet Bey's father owned a stationery shop where Mehmet worked with his brothers for many years. When business dealings resulted in too many family conflicts, Mehmet left the shop to start a business of his own. He found a business for sale in the Burmalı Han, a shop that sold sacks for packing various items, from turmeric to textiles to trash. For over 30 years he has worked long hours in this small shop (from 7 a.m. to 7 p.m.), earning enough to support his family and put his two daughters through university. He enjoys working in the historical area of Eminönü and feels proud to be next door to the lovely Rüstem Paşa Mosque.

TURAN GÖRGÖR
Street Cobbler Corner of Uzunçarşı & İsmetiye Sokak

Turan Görgör's father started a shoe repair business on this corner 50 years ago, and Turan Bey continues in his father's footsteps (pardon the pun). He enjoys working outdoors and even when there's little business, people stop to chat with him over his sewing machine. Each morning he sets up his site in this same spot beside a huge tree. He has a chair, his last (a cobbler's shoe form), and a table that holds his sewing machine and other equipment. On rainy days he sets up an umbrella, and in cold weather Turan Bey keeps a fire going beside him in a mangal (hibachi-type stove). He can usually repair a shoe in minutes, though at times it takes an hour or two, depending on how busy he is. He can be found on this corner nearly every day of the year, except Sunday, of course, a day he devotes to his lovely wife.

AYHAN BULUT
Hamamcı / Süleymaniye Hamamı

Though it's a bit daunting to step into a *hamam*, Ayhan Bulut does his best to soften your discomfort with his winning smile and warm banter. He sits at an elevated desk just inside the door of the main lobby of the *hamam*, taking fees and explaining the process of a *hamam* for the many tourists who visit this newly-renovated *hamam*. A handsome young man, Ayhan Bey enjoys interacting with his guests and learning about their countries as he teases and flirts with them. He said he's worked in the *hamam* for 500 years, although that's a bit questionable—just more of his banter. The Süleymaniye Hamam has been around nearly that long, though, as it was established around 1550. It sat unused for 85 years, reopening to the public in 2002.

ULVİ SERDAR SERÇE
Spice Dealer / Küçük Çukur Han

As you wander down the street between the Çukur Hans (Büyük and Küçük), your nose will lead you to the spice seller's shops (*baharatçı*). Huge tubs and sacks of spices will tickle your nostrils, and you'll be sure to learn a few things about spices by stopping in to visit one of the shop owners. Ulvi Serçe is one of the few who speak English.

Ulvi Bey imports spices from eastern Turkey and as far away as Indonesia and Brazil, then ships them all over the country. Each day he works with his son and another employee from 7 a.m. to 6 p.m., setting out bags and barrels of spices to lure customers into his shop.

Sniff the cinnamon, cloves, pepper grains and nutmeg, then taste a few raisins and black sesame seeds before you leave this haven of sensuous pleasure. If you're a gourmet, you won't be able to leave without purchasing at least a few spices to add to your home pantry (at a far cheaper rate than you'd find in the Spice Bazaar). Remember, the spices are waiting to lure you every day—even on Sunday during busy tourist seasons.

History of Istanbul

Istanbul, (also known as Chalcedon, Byzantion, Deutera Roma, Nea Roma, Byzantium, Constantinople, Konstantiniyye, Stamboul), not only spans two continents, it spans many centuries. Although most of the architecture of the city is less than a thousand years old, its history reaches much further back. This ancient city didn't become officially known as Istanbul until 1928, several years after the Turkish Republic was established, and foreigners still called it Constantinople for thirty years afterward.

The area known as Asia Minor (Anatolia) has a long, rich history, with evidence of civilization dating back to 20,000 B.C. Few people realize that modern Turkey reaches to Mesopotamia, the Fertile Crescent between the Tigris and Euphrates Rivers, both of which have their sources in Turkey. It is generally accepted, in fact, that the world's first city, Çatalhöyük, was in what is now Turkey. It was an urban settlement of 5,000 to 10,000 people in west-central Anatolia (near Konya), with documented artifacts dating from 7000 B.C.

Early History

676 B.C. Chalcedon, a Greek settlement, is established on the Asian shore of the Bosphorus (today's Kadıköy).

667 B.C. The city of Byzantion is established by Byzas, a Greek colonist, after consulting the Oracle at Delphi. This original settlement develops on the acropolis above Saray Point (location of Topkapı Palace), which allows control over commerce to and from the Black Sea. Byzantion becomes famous for its wine and its fisheries.

512 B.C. Byzantion is taken by the Persians (King Darius).

479 B.C. Byzantion is recaptured by the Spartans and becomes part of the Athenian Empire.

356 B.C. The city rebels and wins its independence from the Athenians.

334 B.C. Alexander the Great conquers Anatolia (the Asian side of the Bosphorus).

The Roman Empire

64 B.C. Pompey brings Byzantion into the Roman Empire, bringing the Latin version of its name, Byzantium, into common use.

A.D. 196 Roman Emperor Septimius Severus destroys the city, then rebuilds it, twice its former size.

A.D. 258 The Asian city of Chalcedon is destroyed by the Goths.

A.D. 330 Roman Emperor Constantine establishes Byzantium as the new capital of the Roman Empire, renaming it Constantinople. The city grows rapidly after this change and flourishes under the next few rulers. This expanded Roman Empire later becomes known as the Byzantine Empire.

A.D. 337 Emperor Constantine is baptized a Christian on his deathbed.

A.D. 395 Emperor Theodosius the Great divides the Roman Empire in two, giving the eastern part (including Constantinople) to his son Arcadius and the western part (including Rome) to his son Honorius.

The Eastern Roman Empire, Later Known as the Byzantine Empire (as Greek became the common language)

537   Emperor Justinian dedicates the new Hagia Sophia; his reign is the golden era of the Byzantine Empire.

674   The Arabs begin a five-year siege of Constantinople. They are unsuccessful, and this inability to take the city keeps them from gaining access to Eastern Europe via the Bosphorus.

NOTE ON THE MIDDLE AGES: While cultural development in Europe stagnates through the Dark Ages, Constantinople flourishes as a cultural center—an oasis of education, law, and the arts. The Byzantine Emperors spread Christianity to Russia and the Slavic nations.

The Seljuk Empire

1071   The Seljuk Turks (Muslims) defeat the Byzantine army in Manzikert (Malazgirt in Turkish) and take control of Anatolia (Asia Minor).

The Crusades

1096   The armies of the First Crusade pass through Constantinople and help the emperor retake the Anatolian seaboard from the Seljuk Turks, though the Seljuks retain most of Anatolia.

1204   Enrico Dandolo, a Doge from Venice, diverts the Fourth Crusade to Constantinople, cuts the chain across the Golden Horn, and storms the city. Greek Orthodox churches and monasteries are turned to the Latin rite. The city is stripped of most of its monuments, holy relics and artistic treasures, which are shipped to Western Europe. The city is under Latin rule.

1261   Michael VIII Palaeologus recaptures Constantinople, restoring the Byzantine Empire.

The Ottoman Empire

1299   The Ottoman state is established by Osman I in Bursa along the eastern edge of the Byzantine Empire. The Ottoman state fights to secure the area for the Muslim faith.

1391   Sultan Beyazıt I besieges Constantinople for seven months and builds the Anadolu Hisarı fortress on the Asian side of the Bosphorus.

1400   Sultan Beyazıt I besieges Constantinople for a second time but is again unsuccessful.

1422   Sultan Murat II besieges Constantinople, which has by now been reduced from a great empire to a city-state. His quest is unsuccessful, but his son builds the fortress Rumeli Hisarı on the European shore of the Bosphorus, across from where his great-grandfather had built his fortress, which secures control of the strait.

1453   Sultan Mehmet II takes Constantinople on May 29. This date becomes known as "The Conquest," and Mehmet II is known as "Mehmet the Conqueror" or "Fatih." His first task is to call back all those who have fled, promising to tolerate different religions, allow people to keep their prayer houses, etc. He comes with an army of mercenaries, but he realizes he needs merchants and artisans to rebuild the city. At this time Jews, Christians and Muslims live in harmony in the city. As a part of this, two massive buildings, the Cevahir Bedesteni and Sandal Bedesteni, are built shortly after the conquest. Centuries later, the maze of streets surrounding these bazaars will be covered over to become the Grand Bazaar.

1478	The first stages of Topkapı Palace are completed.
1520–1566	Süleyman the Magnificent brings the Ottoman Empire to its glory, conquering lands from Algiers to the Caspian Sea and from Hungary to the Persian Gulf. His architect, Sinan, builds many of the most awe-inspiring Ottoman buildings, particularly mosques.
1556	Süleymaniye Mosque is completed, one of the most famous of Sinan's mosques.
1616	After seven years of construction, the Blue Mosque is completed.
1622	The Janissaries (royal troops) revolt and murder Osman II in Yedikule Castle.
1727	The first Ottoman printing press with the Arabic alphabet is set up in Istanbul and begins to print texts in Ottoman.
1853	Sultan Abdülmecit I moves the administrative center of the empire from Topkapı Palace to the new Dolmabahçe Palace, a baroque castle fashioned after Versailles and completed in 1856. Because the Ottoman Empire is in decline at this time, the palace is financed by loans from foreign banks.
1883	The Orient Express marks the first rail link between Paris and Constantinople.

The Turkish Republic

1915–1916	Allied forces land at Gallipoli (Gelibolu) but are repulsed by Turkish troops, under the leadership of a young new officer, Mustafa Kemal Paşa.
1919–1922	British and French troops occupy Istanbul.
1919–1922	The Turkish War of Independence is fought against the Greeks.

1922	The Ottoman Empire collapses and the Sultanate is abolished. The country is divided up by the Allies after WWI.
1923	The Treaty of Lausanne establishes the Turkish Republic, setting borders around areas primarily settled by Turks.
1923–1934	Mustafa Kemal Atatürk establishes many reforms to modernize and unite the Turkish republic, including abolishing polygamy, the fez, and the Arabic alphabet, which is replaced by a modified Latin alphabet. He establishes the use of family surnames and grants women equal rights as well as the right to vote. He establishes a secular state by abolishing Islam as the state religion, although he oversees an extensive population exchange between Greece and Turkey as a condition of the Lausanne Treaty (Greek Muslims move to Turkey, while Turkish Greek-Orthodox Christians move to Greece).
1928	The name of Konstantiniyye (Constantinople) is officially changed to Istanbul, although many countries continue to call it Constantinople.
1936	Hagia Sophia becomes a museum.
1938	Atatürk dies in Dolmabahçe Palace.
1973	A suspension bridge uniting European and Asian Turkey, is built across the Bosphorus, on the 50th anniversary of the establishment of the republic.

OTTOMAN SULTANS (1-6 before the Conquest of Constantinople) from: *Osmanlılar Albümü* by Abdülkadir Dedeoğlu

Sultan's name	Father	Mother
1- Osman Gazi	Ertuğrul Gazi	Hayme Hatun
2- Orhan Gazi	Osman Gazi	Mal Hatun
3- Murat I	Orhan Gazi	Nilüfer Hatun
4- "Yıldırım" Beyazıt I	Murat I	Gülçiçek Hatun
5- "çelebi" Mehmet I	Beyazıt I	Devlet Hatun
6- Murat II	Mehmet I	Emine Hatun
7- "Fatih" Sultan Mehmet II	Murat II	Huma Hatun
8- Beyazıt II	Mehmet II	Mükrime Hatun
9- "Yavuz" Sultan Selim I	Beyazıt II	Gülbahar Hatun
10- "Kanuni" Sultan Süleyman	Selim I	Hafsa Hatun
11- Selim II	Süleyman I	Hürrem Sultan
12- Murat III	Selim II	Nurbanu Sultan
13- Mehmet III	Murat III	Safiye Hatun
14- Ahmet I	Mehmet III	Handan Sultan
15- Mustafa I	Murat III	Handan Sultan
16- "Genç" Osman II	Ahmet I	Mahfiruz Sultan
17- Murat IV	Ahmet I	Kösem Sultan
18- İbrahim	Ahmet I	Kösem Sultan
19- Mehmet IV	İbrahim	Turhan Sultan
20- Süleyman II	İbrahim	Saliha Sultan
21- Ahmet II	İbrahim	Hatice Sultan
22- Mustafa II	Mehmet IV	Gülnuş Sultan
23- Ahmet III	Mehmet IV	Gülnuş Sultan
24- Mahmut I	Mustafa II	Saliha Sultan
25- Osman III	Mustafa II	Şehsuvar Sultan
26- Mustafa III	Ahmet III	Mihrimah Sultan
27- Abdülhamit I	Ahmet III	Rabia Sultan
28- Selim III	Mustafa III	Mihrişah Sultan
29- Mustafa IV	Abdülhamit I	Ayşe Sultan
30- Mahmut II	Abdülhamit I	Nakşidil Sultan
31- Abdülmecit	Mahmut II	Bezmialem Sultan
32- Abdülaziz	Mahmut II	Pertevniyal Sultan
33- Murat V	Abdülmecit	Şevkefza Sultan
34- Abdülhamit II	Abdülmecit	Tirimüjgan
35- Mehmet V Reşat	Abdülmecit	Gülcemal
36- Mehmet VI Vahdettin	Abdülmecit	Gülistü

birth – death		reigning years
1258 – 1326		1299 – 1326
1281 – 1360		1326 – 1359
1326 – 1389		1359 – 1389
1360 – 1403	prisoner of Timur	1389 – 1402
1389 – 1421	fought with his brothers	1413 – 1421
1402 – 1451		1421 – 1451
1432 – 1481		1451 – 1481
1447 – 1512	gave up and died	1481 – 1512
1470 – 1520		1512 – 1520
1495 – 1566		1520 – 1566
1524 – 1574		1566 – 1574
1546 – 1595		1574 – 1595
1566 – 1603		1595 – 1603
1590 – 1617		1603 – 1617
1592 – 1639	deposed twice	1617 – 1618, 1622 – 1623
1604 – 1622	killed	1618 – 1622
1612 – 1640		1623 – 1640
1616 – 1648	deposed and killed	1640 – 1648
1642 – 1693	deposed	1648 – 1687
1642 – 1691		1687 – 1691
1643 – 1695		1691 – 1695
1664 – 1704	deposed	1695 – 1703
1673 – 1736	deposed	1703 – 1730
1696 – 1754		1730 – 1754
1699 – 1757		1754 – 1757
1717 – 1774		1757 – 1774
1725 – 1789		1774 – 1789
1761 – 1808	deposed and killed a year later	1789 – 1807
1779 – 1808	deposed and killed	1807 – 1808
1785 – 1839		1808 – 1839
1823 – 1861		1839 – 1861
1830 – 1876	deposed and killed	1861 – 1876
1840 – 1904	deposed	1876 (93 days)
1842 – 1918	deposed	1876 – 1909
1844 – 1918		1909 – 1918
1861 – 1926	deposed	1918 – 1922

Glossary

ağa	honorary title for the chief or master of the sultan's eunuchs or of a military squadron
atelier	artisan's workshop
baroque	a highly ornate architectural style
bas-relief	low relief sculptures where figures project slightly from the background
bedesten	section of a bazaar where valuable goods are kept
caravanserai	inn or han
cevahir	gems or precious stones
corbel	stone structure jutting from a wall
çarşı	bazaar or market
çeşme	fountain
çorap	sock or stocking
çuha	a type of thick cloth
çukur	sunken
dervish	a member of a Muslim religious fraternity who professes extreme poverty
ebru	marbelized paper, literally "cloud" in Persian
elçi	ambassador
eski	old
fatih	conqueror
firman	a sultan's decree
grand vizier	sultan's chief advisor
hamam	Turkish bath
han	inn inside the city walls
harem	separate quarters of the house for Muslim women
imam	the prayer leader in a mosque
imaret	soup kitchen
imperial loge	private prayer place in a mosque reserved for the sultan
Kaaba	a square building that covers the holy Black Stone in Mecca
kapalı	closed or covered
kayık	a long, gondola-like barge
keş	a spinner
kûfi	calligraphy done with angled letters

külliye	mosque complex
lale	tulip
leblebi	roasted chickpeas
marpuç	the mouthpiece of a water pipe
medrese	Theological academy
mektep	primary school
mescit	a small mosque
mihrap	niche of a mosque or prayer room that faces Mecca
minaret	a thin tower attached to a mosque
müezzin	a person who chants the call to prayer from a mosque
nargile	water pipe
Osmanlı	Ottoman
portico	a roof supported by columns
ramatevi	a shop where gold and silver filings are melted together for recrafting
rococo	ornate floral, leafy style of architecture
sabun	soap
saray	palace
sarnıç	cistern, reservoir for storing water
sebil	fountain structure for distributing drinks
sepet	basket
sim	gold or silver thread
sof	woolen cloth or raw silk
sipahi	horseman in the Ottoman army
sülüs	calligraphy done with rounded letters
süpürgeciler	broom sellers
şerefe	the balcony of a minaret
taş	stone
tavla	backgammon
tekke	dervish lodge
tuğra	the sultan's signature or stamp (symbol)
türbe	mausoleum or tomb
ulema	the religious hierarchy of the Ottoman Empire
vezir	vizier; advisor or minister of a sultan
yeni	new
zindan	dungeon

Bibliography

Books:

Dedeoğlu, Abdülkadir. *Osmanlılar Albümü*. Istanbul: Osmanlı Publishing, 1981.

Eyewitness Travel Guides ISTANBUL. New York: DK Publishing, Inc., 2004.

Freely, John. *John Freely's Istanbul*. London: Scala Publishers, Ltd, Northburgh House, 2005.

Freely, John, and Hilary Sumner-Boyd. *Strolling Through Istanbul*. Istanbul, Turkey: Redhouse Press, 1996.

Güran, Ceyhan. *Türk Hanlarının Gelişimi ve İstanbul Hanları Mimarisi*. İstanbul: Vakıflar Genel Müdürlüğü Yayınları, 1976.

Swan, Suzanne (main contributor), *Eyewitness Travel Guides TURKEY*. New York: DK Publishing, Inc., 2003.

Weissenbacher, Edda. *Discovering the Past in Istanbul: The Hans* (4 pamphlets). Istanbul: Weissenbacher Publishing, 1991.

Yale, Pat, Verity Campbell, and Richard Plunkett. *Lonely Planet Turkey*. Footscray, Victoria, Australia: Lonely Planet Publications Pty Ltd, 2003.

Maps:

"Istanbul, Turkey." *Google Maps*. 2007. Google. 4 Oct 2007. <http://maps.google.com/>.

Vlada, Luis A., and Veronica L. "Kapalı Çarşı –Grand Bazaar- since 1461." Istanbul: Özlem Matbaacılık ve Reklamcılık Ltc. Şti.: 1989.

Yaman, Yücel, Yusuf Güven, Murat Onay, Orhan Batmacı, and Mart Matbaası. *Sokak Sokak İstanbul* Kent Atlası. 33rd ed. Istanbul: İki Nokta Bilişim Araştırma Basın Yayın Tic. Ltd., 2003.

Web Sites:

Berger, Albrecht. "Byzantium 1200 Introduction." *Byzantium 1200.* 2004. 4 Oct 2007
  <http://www.byzantium1200.com/introduction.html>.

"Constantinople." *Classic Encyclopedia.* 2006. 4 Oct 2007.
  <http://www.1911encyclopedia.org/Constantinople>.

Cullen, Ellen. "Tourist gets lost in the Grand Bazaar." *Time Out Istanbul*, 30 Aug 2004. 04 Oct 2007.
  <http://www.timeout.com.tr/yazi_phb?artID=47>.

Gamm, Niki. "Grand Bazaar, out on a 500-year-old shopping spree—from where to where?" *The Turkish Daily News* 02 Jul 2003. 4 Oct 2007.
  <http://www.turkishdailynews.com,tr/archives.php?id=32842>.

Hamilton, Kathy. "A peaceful place for *nargile* and carpets." *Zaman*, 20 Jul 2007. 18 Nov 2007.
  <http://www.tourexpi.com/en-tr/news.html~nid=2987>.

"Istanbul Guide—Mosques and Complex." Istanbul. 2005. Istanbul Metropolitan Municipality. 4 Oct 2007.
  <www.ibb.gov.tr/en-US/KenteBakis/IstanbulGuide/MosquesComplex>.

McDonald, John K. "Istanbul's Caravan Stops." *The New York Times*, 17 Apr 1983. 4 Oct 2007.
  <http://query.nytimes.com/gst/fullpage.html?sec=travel&res=9C00EEDD1638F934A25757C0A965948260>.

Tomaselli, Rinaldo. "Liste de han et caravansérails." *Istanbul Guide.* 2006. Istanbul Insolite. 4 Oct 2007.
  <http://www.istanbulguide.net/istguide/artetarch/batimliste/han/index.htm>.

Index

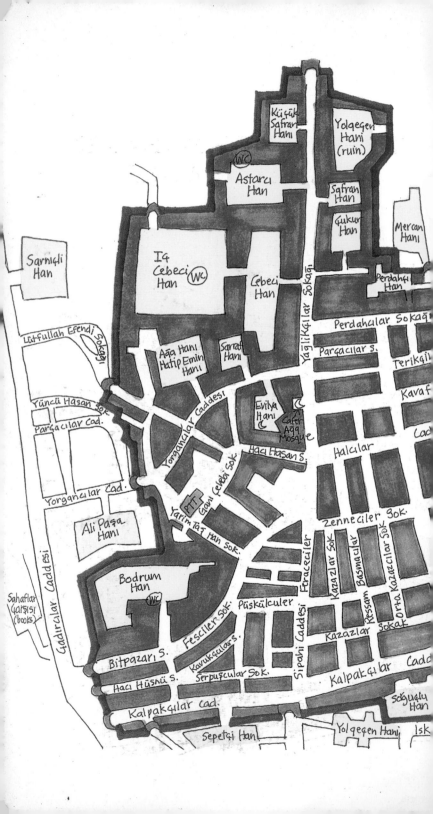